SALTWATER CITY

SALTWATER 鹹塰 CITY

An Illustrated History of
the Chinese in Vancouver

Paul Yee

Douglas & McIntyre, Vancouver/Toronto
University of Washington Press, Seattle

Douglas & McIntyre Ltd.
1615 Venables Street
Vancouver, British Columbia
Canada V5L 2H1

The assistance of the Multiculturalism Canada Program, Secretary of State,
in publishing this book is gratefully acknowledged.

Canadian Cataloguing in Publication Data

Yee, Paul Richard, 1956–
Saltwater City

Includes index.
ISBN 0-88894-616-3

1. Chinatown (Vancouver, B.C.) – History. 2. Chinese
– British Columbia – Vancouver – History. 3. Chinese
Canadians – British Columbia – Vancouver – History.
4. Vancouver (B.C.) – History. I. Title.
FC3847.9C5Y43 1988   971.1'33   C88-091369-X
F1089.7.C5Y43 1988

Published simultaneously in the United States of America by the
University of Washington Press, Seattle, Washington.

Library of Congress Cataloging-in-Publication Data

Yee, Paul
Saltwater City : The Chinese in Vancouver / Paul Yee.
p. cm.
Includes index.
ISBN 0-295-96701-3 (University of Washington Press)
1. Chinese – British Columbia – Vancouver – History. 2. Vancouver
(B.C.)–History. I. Title.
F1089.5.V22Y44 1988
971.1'33—dc19   88-20717 CIP

Design:
RayMahDesign,Inc.
Typeset:
Vancouver Typesetting Co. Ltd.
Printed and bound in Canada:
D.W. Friesen & Sons Ltd.

CONTENTS

6

Dedicated to Michael and Jennifer, the fourth generation of my family to be in Canada.

Saltwater City was the name that the early Chinese gave Vancouver to differentiate it from the older mainland city of New Westminster by the freshwater Fraser River. But that name, Hahm-sui-fau, is now rarely used; the sound-alike Wen-go-wa is Vancouver's Chinese name.

In the intervening years, much more than the name has changed. The Chinese came here before Vancouver was incorporated, and the story of their over one hundred years in the city has never before been fully told. Today there are those who speak no English and those who speak no Chinese. The early peasant settlers and their third- and fourth-generation descendants have been displaced in number by sophisticated urbanites from Hong Kong and other cities. Different dialects and languages swirl through Chinatown. Chinese Canadians identify themselves by their place in history; they call themselves old-timers, native-born, came-in-1969, or fourth-generation. And the Chinese terms for old-timers (*loh-wah-kew*) and native-borns (*to-seng*) are proudly flaunted.

To read the history of Vancouver's Chinese Canadians is to better understand the broader history of Vancouver and of Canada itself. For many aspects of social history have not found their way into textbooks or popular histories, and primary among them are the experiences of non-English-speaking and visible-minority immigrants. This is particularly true when it comes to appreciating the much longer history of the Chinese presence in western as compared to eastern Canada. *Saltwater City* attempts to facilitate that appreciation. Out of this history rises a recurring question: How do we treat those who are different? White Canada once despised the Chinese, while Canadian-borns have resented the foreign-born.

This book pays tribute to those who went through the hard times, to those who swallowed their pride, to those who were powerless and humiliated, but who still carried on. They all had faith that things would be better for future generations. They have been proven correct.

This book grew out of the *Saltwater City* exhibition mounted by the Chinese Cultural Centre (CCC) to celebrate Vancouver's Centennial in 1986, so I must thank the CCC for sponsoring that project and the Exhibition Committee for organizing it. It was during one of our planning meetings that editor Denise Bukowski advised us about a publication for the exhibition. She looked at the research outline for the show and said, "I think you've got a book here."

My greatest thanks go to the people who consented to be interviewed, who lent photographs for the book, and who made introductions. Without them, this book would not exist. They are: Audrey Bragagnolo, Rev. Len Burnham of the Chinese United Church, Glenn Burwell,

Corrine Chan, Donna Chan, Dr. Ted Chang, Mrs. Yat Leong Chang, Julie Chen, Selina Chew, Harry Chin, the Chinese Benevolent Association, Raymond Chow, Leila Chu, Dr. William and Patrice Chu, Dr. Wallace Chung, Janice Clarfield, Geoff Crawford, Pearl and Gordon Cumyow, Sister Theresa Fung, Jimmy Hing, Mimie Ho, Sue Gee Jackman, Wendy Jang, Andy Joe, Linda Joe, Mrs. Jung, Anna Lam, Wah Bong Lam, Nelly Law, A. Jack Lee, Art Lee, Carol Lee, Charles Lee, Ian Lee, Victor Lee, Celia Leung, Raymond Leung, Harold Lim, Herbert Lim, Anne and Wing Loo, Mrs. Git Fong Louie, Tong Louie, Jimmy Lum, Raymond Lum, Tommy Ming Lum, Victor Lum, Bill Mah, Roy Mah, Ramona Mar, Mon Keang Chinese School, Dora Nipp, Charlie San, Chuck Seto, Rev. C. C. Shiu, Ron Shon, Joan Sien, Romy So, Duncan Stacey, Tommy Tao, S. Yim Tse, Sandra Wilking, Alfred K. Wong, Bill and Jack Wong, Chimpo Wong of the Hon Hsing Athletic Association, Frank Wong, Jack and Nancy Wong, Kown Fow Wong, Larry Wong, Robert S. Wong, Shupon Wong, Bill Yee, Elsie Yet, Dick Yip, Henry Yip, Kew Gin Yip, Mary Yip, Victoria Yip, George Yipp, Elwin Yuen, Harry Yuen, Mr. Wing Chong Yuen.

Writing can be a lonely occupation, and I have special thanks for Judy Chan, Patrice Chu, Ian Lee, Larry Wong, Jim Wong-Chu, and Victoria Yip who were supportive in different and special ways.

I am grateful to Hayne Wai and Bennett Lee for their comments on the manuscript.

Thanks must also be extended to Sue Baptie and the staff of the Vancouver City Archives who encouraged me to undertake this project. Chris Middlemass and Laurie Robertson of the Historic Photographs Division of the Vancouver Public Library offered valuable help, as did John K. Wong of the Chinese Cultural Centre and Seline So of the Chinese Community Library Services Association. I also received help from George Brandak and the staff at Special Collections of the University of British Columbia Library, Ivan Sayers and Henry Tabbers of the Vancouver Museum, Len McCann of the Vancouver Maritime Museum, the Vancouver School Board, and Bob Turner and Bob Griffiths of the Royal British Columbia Museum.

Funding for the research and writing of this book came from the Canada Council and from the Multiculturalism Program of the Department of Secretary of State of Canada.

The Pearl River teemed with life at Guangzhou. These boats housed a floating population of several hundred thousand and lined the riverbanks for several miles.

Before Saltwater: From Old World to New

Cultural baggage. Portrait of Zhang Tian Shi, the "Catcher of Ghosts." A charm used to protect the home.

When Vancouver incorporated in 1886, two trends in Chinese-Canadian history were already established. One was the position of the Chinese in the local economy, and the other was the racial hostility hurled at them. To understand both of them it is necessary to explore the historical and cultural background of the first Chinese immigrants, and their experiences in Canada before Vancouver was founded.

They came from eight rural counties in the Pearl River delta in Guangdong province on the southeast coast of China. Guangzhou (Canton), at the Pearl River's mouth, had been a major port city since the eighth century A.D., and in 1757 it became the sole Chinese port to trade with the West. News about New World opportunities came readily to nearby peasants. In addition, Guangdong's tropical climate provided a long growing season and plentiful cash crops, sold at local market towns. This economy created money-wise and mobile peasants.

Southern merchants and artisans travelled to other cities without their families, but kept strong ties to home. Travellers formed mutual help clubs to provide housing, letters of introduction, and credit. Sons borne by host city wives or concubines were often sent back to their fathers' villages. When emigration to North America started, the people of south China had already learned how to survive away from home and loved ones.

Upheaval in China

In the mid-nineteenth century massive problems struck China. Between 1787 and 1850 Guangdong's population almost doubled from sixteen to twenty-eight million, yet no agricultural innovations emerged to increase the food supply. Land ownership was concentrated in a few hands, so peasant-tenants faced rising rents and taxes. Wage-labour jobs became scarce after China's defeat in the First Opium War (1839-42), when four new treaty ports were opened. These diverted trade activity away from Guangzhou and put many people out of work. As well, the lower prices of foreign manufactured goods undercut native Chinese products.

Economic troubles were compounded by a breakdown in law and order. The Taiping Rebellion swept through China between 1850 and 1864 and claimed twenty million lives. Other uprisings erupted in the Pearl River delta in 1853 and took an estimated one million lives. Fighting over land and water rights in several Pearl River counties cost 150,000 lives between 1854 and 1868. Ongoing warfare prevented farmers from maintaining their fields when able-bodied men were conscripted for military service. Banditry and piracy continued unabated under the weakened central government. The peasants also faced natural disasters such as flood and drought.

These crises forced many

Stores along a street in Guangzhou, the ancient trading city. The signs here advertised a money exchanger, a shop that mounted paintings, and stores selling straw mats, rattan, bedding, screens and netting, and furniture.

Guangdong residents to emigrate. Those who went to North America were almost entirely men: merchants, peasants, and labourers. The merchants were few in number, and most came from Sam-yup, the commercially advanced Three Counties surrounding Guangzhou. They took capital abroad to establish stores selling groceries and supplies to their compatriots. They also had connections to established trading houses in Hong Kong and Guangzhou.

The majority of the migrants, however, came from Say-yup, the Four Counties. They included landless hired hands, sharecroppers, and small land-holders. Some had worked in cities and ports as pedlars, rice carriers, and boatmen, or had plied trades such as cobbling. Those who owned land often sold it to raise passage money, while other families pooled resources to send one clan member abroad.

Cultural Baggage

Despite their different economic backgrounds, the emigrants shared similar values. Confucianism taught that in a harmonious society, all people accepted their station in life and gave unquestioning obedience to authority. Peasants were idealized as sturdy and virtuous yeomen with a simple, reverent attachment to the land; in reality, they lived at a subsistence level.

The gentry class of scholars and landowners acted as an informal government in the countryside. Merchants, although ranked lowest in

the Confucian order, were not social
outcasts; they were viewed as useful and
valuable members of society. Merchant
families moved up into the gentry in two
ways: they purchased low-ranking
official titles, or they hired good tutors
to prepare their sons for the imperial
examinations.

Confucianism emphasized the
family as key to peace, order, and good
government in society. Family harmony
and stability depended on the respect
paid to the oldest living male. As in
other preindustrial societies, the
Chinese family was an economic unit,
keen to enrich itself, protect its
interests, and enhance future prospects.

In south China, family power was
expressed through the lineage or clan, a
network of families possessing a
common surname and a common
founding ancestor. In Guangdong many
villages held only a few surnames, and
in Say-yup many villages contained only
one surname. The lineages were
Guangdong's largest landowners. They
collected rents, loaned money,
underwrote lawsuits, dispensed relief
for the aged and needy, and maintained
public buildings and bridges.

These lineage activities gave
individual peasants a strong sense of
cohesion, of belonging to a larger social
unit. A wealthy, powerful lineage
supplied prestige to all its members,
rich and poor alike. The lineage was
also important for upward mobility
because it paid the costs of the
government exams. Accordingly,

Dragon Head Ring village in Zhongshan
county in Guangdong province. The gun
tower (*centre*) was built to protect peasants
from roving bandits. Often, money remitted
by overseas emigrants financed the
construction of such towers.

Chinese pedlar, British Columbia, c. 1885.
The shoulder pole was commonly used in
China for the quick transport of goods by
foot.

Mealtime for Chinese immigrants
aboard ship, late nineteenth century.
This is a rare image, because few photos

were taken of *any* immigrant group
during the voyage to the New World.

12

Form of Contract Passage Ticket.

individuals were urged to contribute to the wealth and well-being of their lineage. Overseas Chinese sent money home not only to feed their families but also to strengthen the lineage. The cultural baggage they brought to the New World thus helped them survive in a hostile environment.[1]

The Chinese Come to British Columbia

"They are generally abused, and yet everybody employs them."
Sir Matthew Begbie, 1885[2]

The first Chinese came to British Columbia in 1858 from California, where they had worked for a decade. Two years later, more sailed directly from China. These latter and all subsequent newcomers had no mining experience, but they followed the surge of eager gold-seekers north and east into the province with their gold-pans and shovels and weigh-scales. By 1863 four thousand Chinese were working in the Cariboo.[3]

The Chinese had a unique mining strategy: they reworked sites that whites had abandoned. One reason for this was that used claims were easier (and sometimes cheaper) to acquire than new ones. Another was the reception that the Chinese met in the New World. In California, they had been beaten, robbed, and kicked off their claims by hostile whites, and British Columbia was not free from such incidents. At Hope, a mob of California miners tried to stop Chinese steamer passengers from disembarking and threatened them

with violence.[4] In the Cayoosh region, whites shot two Chinese in a dispute over a claim.[5] At Forks City, whites threatened to drive out the Chinese.[6] Not surprisingly, the Chinese kept a safe distance from the frenzied first-strike areas of the gold rush.

Of nearly two thousand gold miners in the province in 1883, almost fifteen hundred were Chinese. About them the inland revenue inspector commented: "The larger number of claims in the province are owned and worked by Chinese, their more frugal habits, their greater industry and more moderate expectations of reward making profitable to them claims that the white miners regard as not having sufficient attraction. Thus, but for the Chinese, the production of gold in this country would not reach nearly the sum shown."[7]

The Chinese eagerly filled other gaps in the frontier economy. They serviced the largely male populations of the gold rush with laundries, restaurants, and vegetable farms. The Cariboo Wagon Road, started in 1863 between Harrison Lake and Williams Lake, used about a thousand Chinese workers.[8] After it was completed, they worked as teamsters, driving horse teams through the dangerous canyons. In 1866 Western Union employed some five hundred Chinese to string telegraph wires between New Westminster and Quesnel.[9] In the 1870s fish canneries were established along the British Columbia coast, and Chinese workers

A Chinese work gang by the Canadian Pacific Railway tracks, at a camp between Glacier House and the Loop, just west of Rogers Pass, 1889.

Reward! Violence on the frontier. From *Inland Sentinel,* 17 May 1883

The Railway Riot,

In our last issue a telegram reported serious trouble at Hautier's Station, near Lytton; we have endeavored to find out particulars, and from the account to hand it would appear that on Monday of last week a man named J. Gray, in charge of a gang of Chinamen, numbering 28, notified the Chinese bookman that two of the number was not working as they should, and they were not wanted any more. That evening the bookman again saw Gray and told him they would do better and asked that they be tried longer. Next day when the young man acting as timekeeper went his rounds the bookman gave in the full number of men, 28, but when Foreman Gray made his report only 26 were given in. The timekeeper stated the difference, and went back to the bookman, who insisted that Gray said the two objectionable men might work again. This the Foreman stoutly denied, and the bookman then wanted credit for them for a quarter of a day up to that hour 9 a. m., and he would send them away. This the Foreman refused and the bookman urged the timekeeper to enter the quarter of a day, and upon refusal the bookman grew angry and the timekeeper picked up a stone as he thought he discovered a speck of war. The Chinamen working close by grew boisterous and threatening, and it is stated the timekeeper struck the bookman with the stone. The lifting up of the stone is admitted but using it denied. At this point J. M. Hayes, bridge boss, came to the front, and a general row commenced, A teamster named Perry hearing the tumult and witnessing what he considered the danger of his white friends seized a pickhandle and waded in, striking Chinamen right and left. The result was a scattering of the belligerants, and upon examination some of the Chinamen, especially, were considerably injured. Quite once more restored the Chinamen went to their camp, and news was sent to Lytton. Officer Hussey soon arrived from Lytton, and there was found one Chinaman badly injured. Of course there were conflicting accounts of the trouble. All appeared quieted down and it was thought the next day would find work going on as usual.

However, it is stated that about 10 o'clock that night a white man rapped at the Chinese camp and the bookman appearing at the door was told by the untimely visitor that he was to be the Foreman of the gang hereafter and he wanted all to be on hand promptly next morning. After remaining a few minutes he withdrew and pretty soon the bookman heard and saw a number of men, about 20 he thinks, rushing down upon the camp, and all had sticks in their hands. The Chinamen were soon out of their beds and while trying to escape got roughly handled; some knocked down and others running from the blows

The Wah Chong Laundry was operating in 1884 even before Vancouver became a city. It sat on the south side of Water Street, midway between Abbott and Carrall streets, and faced the waters of Burrard Inlet directly.

dominated cannery work because labour shortages still plagued the new province.[10] Engineer and Member of Parliament Edgar Dewdney said in 1879, "In a country where there are mining operations starting up in every direction, you cannot depend on the white labor; they run off to the mines and leave the employer in the lurch, and the only labor they can depend upon is the Chinese."[11]

On Vancouver Island, the Chinese worked as coal miners. Victoria contained the first Chinatown in British Columbia and was a major Chinese centre until after the century's turn. Chinese houseboys were first used there by genteel American settlers, and one employer noted that "Without Chinese servants, the privations in family life, extreme and of wearying monotony, would have become intolerable, and a general exodus of families would have been the result."[12]

Building the Railway

The construction of the British Columbia section of the Canadian Pacific Railway (CPR) sparked the next major influx of Chinese. Between 1881 and 1885 seventeen thousand Chinese came to Canada and many worked on the railway. They received a dollar a day, one-half the wage paid to whites. In gangs of thirty they cleared and graded the roadbed and secured the rail ties with gravel.

Conservative estimates say that six hundred Chinese died during the

construction of the CPR. Landslides and careless dynamite blasts killed many of them. Others died because of primitive living quarters (especially in winter), poor nutrition, and inadequate medical care. In 1891 the Chinese Consolidated Benevolent Association of Victoria retrieved more than three hundred unidentified corpses along the Fraser and Thompson rivers and sent them to China for a proper burial.[13]

When the Canadian Pacific Railway was finished, Saltwater City sprang up at the western end of the transcontinental line. At the same time, the completion of the line put hundreds of Chinese out of work. Some drifted east towards the prairies, some came to Vancouver, and others went back to China.

The first major law seeking to limit Chinese immigration to Canada was enacted once the railroad neared completion. For years there had been strident calls from white British Columbians to restrict the entry and activities of the Chinese. They were accused of driving out white labour and pushing down wages because they worked at lower rates. The Knights of Labour charged: "Chinese labor is of a low degraded and servile type, the result of whose employment in competition with free white labor is to lower and degrade the latter. Their standard of living is reduced to the lowest possible point, and being without family ties, they are enabled to not only live but to grow rich on wages far below

New Schedule of Wages. From *Inland Sentinel*, 15 December 1881

Household servants: a houseboy holding
hand-iron sits with two cooks at New
Westminster, 1868.

Anti-Chinese legislation passed by B.C. legislature.

the lowest minimum at which we can possibly exist."[14]

The Chinese were seen to be disease-ridden and morally and physically inferior to whites. They were charged with impeding economic growth because they sent remittances home instead of spending and investing locally. Legislators, newspapers, organized labour, and the general public all denounced the Chinese. John Robson, the provincial secretary, commented: "I consider their habits are as filthy as their morals, in both eating, drinking and sleeping. They sleep in beds not fit for dogs and live in dirty hovels, so how can they be clean at all?"[15]

Many pieces of restrictive anti-Chinese legislation were passed by the provincial government, but Ottawa disallowed them. Finally, the federal Chinese Immigration Act of 1885 blocked Chinese immigrants with two obstacles that ensured that large numbers of Chinese could not come over. They were forced to pay a head tax of fifty dollars to enter Canada, and no inbound ship could carry more than one Chinese per fifty tons. Immigration dropped in 1886 and 1887 to 212 and 124 respectively, but by 1890 annual arrivals numbered over a thousand again as migrants found means of raising additional funds to pay the head tax.

Dr. J. S. Helmcken, who arrived at Vancouver Island in 1850, told the first Royal Commission on Chinese

Immigration in 1885 that "The Chinese have cultivated the soil, raised vegetables, are employed in tanneries and at the canneries, in boot and shoe making, some in coal and gold mining and other labors. Having done these things, they have benefited the country. They have been producers—the one thing the country stands in need of."[16]

Early morning on Pender Street, looking west towards Carrall Street. Chinese vegetable farmers bring in their produce to sell to pedlars who will take them from door to door, 1904.

Early Chinatown: Putting Down Roots

Two years before Vancouver was incorporated in April of 1886, a count around Burrard Inlet had tallied 114 Chinese, including 60 sawmill hands, 30 washermen/cooks, 10 store clerks, 5 merchants, 5 children, 3 married women, and 1 prostitute. Twenty-five years after incorporation Saltwater City was home to 120,000 people, and its Chinatown had grown from 100 people to 3500 and from a few wooden shacks to several blocks of brick buildings. The streets and alleys were lined with stores of every kind that comprised the new trading hub of Canada's Chinese. It was a community of established families and businesses that set down deep roots and cultivated lofty ambitions.

Chinatown thrived because Saltwater City thrived. The city's harbour, industries, and rail yards drew labourers, merchants, and families to the west. The growing city needed Chinese workers and its transportation network moved Chinese goods throughout the province.

Racial Hostility Begins

Vancouver's growth surged after 1885 when discharged railway workers drifted into the region and found work at the Hastings Sawmill at the foot of Dunlevy Street. When white workers there went on strike in April of 1886 to reduce their working hours, mill manager R. H. Alexander publicly denounced them as "North American Chinamen," meaning that they should not expect to be treated any differently from other workers in the frontier economy. Two weeks later, Alexander ran unsuccessfully for mayor of the new city in its first election. His Chinese workmen got their first taste of Vancouver hospitality when they were chased away from the poll by whites.

Vancouver's newspapers warned that the Chinese presence in the city's business section would lower property values and urged that the Chinese be kept out of the city. After the Great Fire of June 1886 destroyed Vancouver, three street meetings passed resolutions against allowing the Chinese to re-establish themselves. In November a white workers' group known as the Knights of Labour began a campaign to evict the Chinese from Vancouver. They ordered stores not to hire Chinese people or sell them food and supplies. Any store defying the boycott found a big white X painted on its sidewalk.

Mob violence erupted in January of 1887 when a contract to clear the West End forest was let and contractor John MacDougall arrived with twenty Chinese workers. A crowd of 250 whites tramped out to the site, ripped the shacks apart, and hustled the crew down to the docks. There, a hastily passed hat collected twenty-eight dollars, and the workers were shipped off to Victoria. The Chinese lost several hundred dollars' worth of property. The next day, eighteen Chinese living near False Creek were "persuaded" to leave. MacDougall returned shortly with

In 1896, 6,000 local Chinese greeted China's statesman Li Hung Chang at the docks and asked him to negotiate a reduction in the $50 head tax to gain entry into Canada.

another crew of twenty-four Chinese and set up camp again. In the snowy darkness of 24 February, another mob charged up to the camp. They tore down the shacks and burned the workers' bedding and clothing. The Chinese were "badly kicked and knocked about." Next morning, the whites marched into Chinatown with hired wagons. All Chinese were loaded aboard and sent off to New Westminster. But in two weeks' time the Chinese were back, and back to stay.[1]

The First Workers

Despite such incidents, jobs abounded for the Chinese in the new city. Landowners wanted their property cleared of forest to be sold to house-hungry newcomers. But clearing land was expensive: it cost between fifty and three hundred dollars an acre.[2] Chinese workers were the cheapest to use. They were assembled by English-speaking Chinese contractors and they worked independently or with white foremen.

The Chinese middlemen organized

A Chinese houseboy, c. 1900.

Our First Civic Election: For Whites Only

Vancouver's charter of 1886 specifically barred Chinese and Native Indians from voting in the municipal elections. But in the city's first election, R. H. Alexander, manager of the Hastings Mill where many Chinese worked, ran for the mayor's seat. He decided to send his Chinese employees to the poll.

William Gallagher, one of

many real estate dealers who had flocked to the new city, watched the day's proceedings and later told this story to J. S. Matthews, the city archivist, in 1931:

The Chinamen—and their pigtails came on up Hastings Road, lined on both sides with bushes, came on up in twos and threes, some on the road, some on the two-plank sidewalk. Then someone shouted "Here's the

1921   VANCOUVER INCORPORATION.   CHAP. **55**
(Second Session)

(7.) Where real property is leased, rented, or occupied by two or more persons, and is assessed at an amount sufficient, if equally divided between them, to give a qualification to each, then each shall be entitled to be entered on the voters' list and vote in respect of such qualification; otherwise no one shall be entitled to vote in respect of such property.   *Where joint ownership, etc., each person may qualify.*

(8.) No Chinaman, Hindu, Japanese, or Indian shall be entitled to vote at any municipal election for Mayor, Aldermen, Park Commissioners, School Trustees, or any other elective official of any governing or administrative body or board of the city, or to vote on by-laws requiring the assent of the electors.   *No Chinese, Hindu, Japanese, or Indian to vote.*

(9.) In the case of a corporation voting through its authorized agent as hereinbefore provided, such agent shall be entitled to vote on behalf of such corporation from year to year, until his authorization shall be cancelled and notice of such cancellation filed with the City   *Corporation voting through authorized agent.*

From the Vancouver Charter, 1886.

Officers and crew aboard the
Empress of Japan.

crews for mills and logging camps; in 1907 fifteen hundred Chinese in Saltwater City worked in shingle mills. The contractors also sent men to work as cooks and servants in homes, hotels, logging camps, and on coastal steamships. On the Canadian Pacific Empress liners they toiled as cabin boys and firemen. Because of the early shortage of female help, Chinese houseboys were widely used. By the century's turn, 260 Chinese worked as domestics in Vancouver. Private homes paid ten to thirty dollars a month; wages at hotels and camps were higher.[3]

The classic explanation for anti-Chinese racism at the time was that Chinese labourers worked for lower pay, thereby inviting the wrath of displaced white workers. But it was the contract system of hiring Chinese workers that fostered this inequity. The brick industry, for example, once used all-white crews, but by 1900 it employed mostly Chinese. A brickyard owner would go to a Chinese contractor and pay him to round up a crew, because the

Chinamen," and that started it.

There were a lot of navvies around Granville for election day; rough customers from the railroad gangs and bush fellers from the CPR clearing, and they shouted at the approaching Chinamen, and began to move towards them. Then one or two of the Chinamen decided, I suppose, that they did not like the look of things, and that they did not want to vote anyhow, and turned around,

then one or two more came to a standstill, the rest came on up, until there was a little crowd of them, standing, and the white men advancing towards them. The white men shouted at the Chinamen and the Chinamen turned and ran.

Charlie Queen, who drove the stage between here and New Westminster, was sitting on his seat—up on the driver's seat. He shouted too, then whipped up his four horses,

Newspaper rendition of the chase,
Vancouver *Province.*

and roars, and takes off after the Chinamen, stage horses and all, roaring as he went. There was a mighty clatter with Charlie roaring and the stage rattling down the road—a terrific noise, and the Chinamen went faster; so did Charlie and his stage. He chased them all the way to the Hastings Mill, and the Chinamen never stopped running till they got there.

J. S. Matthews faithfully

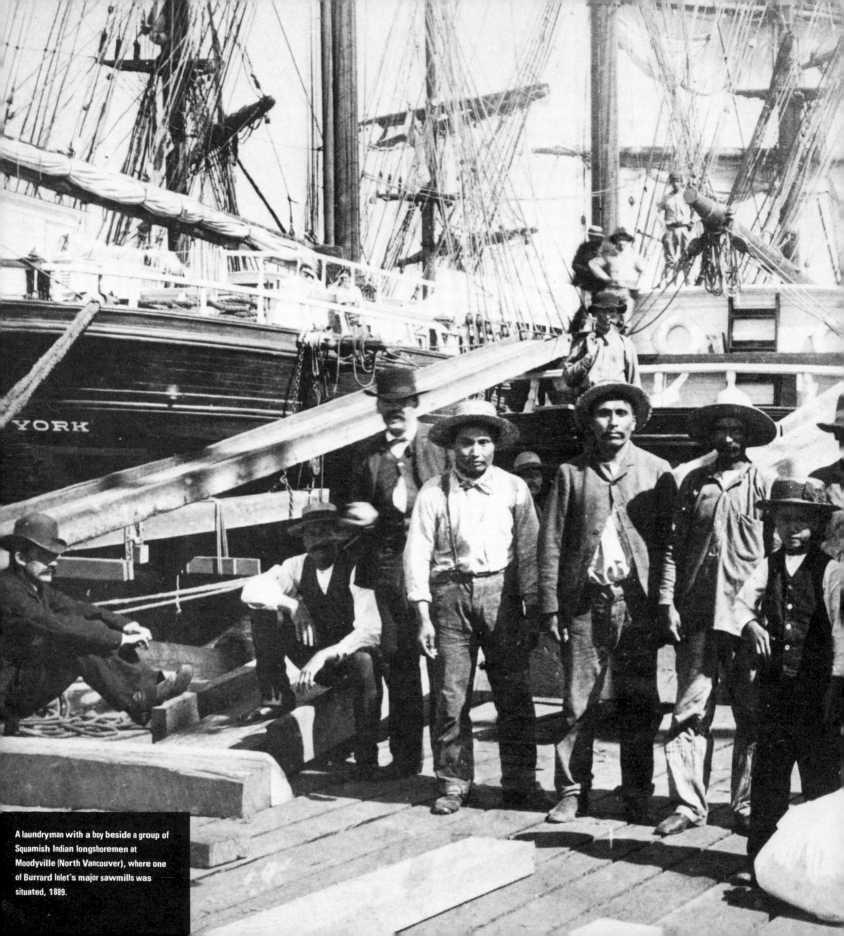

A laundryman with a boy beside a group of Squamish Indian longshoremen at Moodyville (North Vancouver), where one of Burrard Inlet's major sawmills was situated, 1889.

This view of Chinese and Japanese immigrants arriving in Vancouver may have been taken in 1902, with troops from the Hong Kong Regiment, Punjabis, and the Hong Kong Volunteers en route to London to celebrate Queen Victoria's Diamond Jubilee.

employer could not communicate in Chinese. These workers had to promise to buy all their supplies from the contractor. George Gill, a brickyard foreman, told the 1902 Royal Commission on Chinese and Japanese Immigration why:

For every sack of rice [the Chinese contractor] supplied to the camp he charged one dollar more than the retail price of rice in Vancouver. On every pound of pork he supplied he had a profit of about seven cents a pound and he sold to those men about 200 pounds of pork every five days. He supplied tobacco, opium and liquors imported from China. He allowed gambling in the camp and charged each man ten cents per month for the privilege of gambling.[4]

A contractor could bid low for a contract and pay out wages above the amount of the contract, then recover funds from the sale of supplies. White workers, on the other hand, were never required to submit to such organization; they were free agents hired directly

noted that ''Mr. Gallagher laughed at the recollection.'' R. H. Alexander, incidentally, did not win the election.[14]

Washboard Wars

Saltwater City's Chinese laundrymen faced tough times during the early years. The issues were sanitation, competition, and racism.

In 1893 city hall proclaimed that wash-houses could only be built in Chinatown, on Pender Street between Carrall and Columbia. Officials hoped that this restriction would contain the health problem linked to pools of undrained

Chinese laundry, 1902.

water. However, over half the city's Chinese laundries were already working outside the zone, and these stayed in business. It was hard to enforce the bylaw, and by 1900 only two of the city's thirty-six Chinese laundries were found in Chinatown.

By then, competitors had arrived. City hall enlarged the laundry zone to let white-owned steam laundries open downtown, and extended

Seamster, 1889. While the sewing factories of eastern Canada used female workers, Chinatown's labour force was mostly male.

Chinese women, however, did the handwork such as featherstitching.

by the employer with no obligation to buy from him. Brickyard worker Sam Lum's testimony at the same commission described a life typical for Chinese labourers in the region's seasonal industries:

> *I get two dollars a day, a dollar fifty in winter. I only have about six months' work in the year; sometimes we get two days in the week, sometimes none at all. My wife and children are in China; I have never been back. I send thirty or forty dollars home every year. I board myself; there is a house in the brickyard. At present there are only three or four living there, but sometimes twenty live there. It costs me fifteen to sixteen dollars a month to live, two dollars for rice, eight dollars for meat, nine dollars for beer and whiskey.*[5]

Other historians argue that economics was not the sole reason behind anti-Chinese racism because Chinese and white workers did not compete directly for the same jobs in an economy where jobs were race-specific. Instead, racism expressed the yearnings

---

municipal control of washing practices. The new law ruled that clothing being ironed could not be dampened with water sprayed from the mouth; overnight onsite sleeping was banned; no washing, drying, or airing of clothes within sixty feet of any street was allowed; and a separate room for sorting clothing was required. These regulations hit out at the many small, confined operations that the Chinese had started with

minimal capital.

The white-owned steam laundries were mechanized factories that specialized in high-volume bulk washing for hotels and restaurants, as opposed to the personal laundry done by the Chinese. Still, white owners complained about competing against lower Chinese wages, but the Chinese protested that they were not reaping great profits. Two Chinese testified in 1904

that after paying employees and expenses, they earned fifteen to twenty dollars a month. Nevertheless, the health inspector also called for compulsory smallpox vaccination of Chinese laundry workers, the police chief was instructed to enforce Sunday observance laws against the Chinese, and all Chinese who slept at their laundries were registered as lodging-house keepers so that they would fall

under housing regulations.

The laundrymen fought back. Thirty Chinese hired lawyer Wilson V. Senkler and had the lodging-house registration removed. In 1901 real estate agent A. A. Boak petitioned city hall on behalf of his Chinese clients without success to repeal the ban on drying clothes in the open air. When the laundry licence fee was raised to fifty dollars in 1904, Chinese laundrymen

went back to court. Their solicitor, J. A. Russell, alleged that the unreasonably high fees restricted free competition. Moreover, he pointed out to aldermen Stewart and Wilson, who held interests in steam laundries, that ''it might be to their interest if the Chinamen were driven out of the trade by the imposition of this large fee.'' His request was rejected, but the laundrymen tried again the following year.

Meanwhile, working conditions inside the trade prompted a different battle. Laundry employees worked seven days a week, from 6 A.M. to midnight. May of 1906 saw the formation of the Sai Wah Tong, the Chinese Laundry Workers Union, which pressed for a thirteen-hour workday with two hours for meals, and no Sunday labour. At first, the ninety-member union claimed success, but soon it said that

bosses were luring members away with promises of high wages. A bilingual poster appeared in Chinatown, listing seventeen men who denied union membership. Then Wong Cheung Him, one of the seventeen, tore down the poster because he said he had never quit the union. There is no record of what eventually happened to the union or the laundry workers.[15]

The 1907 Riot

It started out as a parade, but turned into an ugly riot. On the hot, sultry evening of Saturday, 7 September 1907, Vancouver's Asiatic Exclusion League staged a parade to call for an end to Asian immigration to Canada. The league had two thousand members, with some three hundred professionals and merchants. Fraternal organizations, ex-servicemen, and the

A Chinese funeral procession crossing Pender Street and heading south on Main Street towards Mountain View Cemetery, 1895. Elaborate parades were held only upon the passing of notable persons in Chinatown.

of white British Columbians for a racially homogenous home. They feared that nonwhites would destroy their capacity to perpetuate their values and traditions, and therefore condemned them as inferior, dangerous, and unalterably alien.[6]

Many Chinese worked for themselves. Whites leased land to them free in exchange for land-clearing services, and by the turn of the century 130 Chinese farmers were supplying the city with fresh vegetables. They also ran pig ranches at the head of False Creek near today's China Creek Park. By 1890 sixteen Chinese laundries were operating in Vancouver,[7] and between 1906 and 1912 nine new laundries started each year, each one situated farther and farther away from Chinatown. In these new neighbourhoods, residents often complained to city hall about Chinese laundries devaluing their properties and asked that licences be witheld.

The Beginning of Chinatown

Chinatown sprang up on the shores of False Creek (which then flowed up to Pender Street) along Carrall, the main street leading to Gastown, the downtown heart of the new city. Early Chinatown's two-storey wooden buildings, frontier style with flat false fronts, were leased from whites by Chinese general merchants. Their shops served as gathering places where people retrieved messages, sent remittances to China, dropped in for conversation, or found temporary shelter if they were passing through or newly arrived. Many general stores started as headquarters for labour contractors, so customers looking for work were naturally attracted to them.

Most of British Columbia's Chinese were scattered throughout the province, so Vancouver became the point of transshipment for goods from China. This meant jobs for bookkeepers, porters, and clerks in Chinatown. By 1900, in addition to some sixty businesses, Chinatown had acquired

Won Alexander Cumyow was the first Chinese born in Canada, at Fort Douglas at the head of Harrison Lake in 1861. He grew up in New Westminster, studied law, and was appointed court interpreter in 1888. Cumyow spoke Native Indian Chinook and several Chinese dialects, including Hakka.

city's fifty-eight trade unions all publicly supported the event.

With a brass band playing patriotic airs, the parade travelled up to the old city hall at Main and Hastings for a series of inflammatory anti-Asian speeches. Eight or nine thousand whites had gathered, but only two thousand could fit into the hall. From time to time, speakers came out of city hall to address them.

The crowds drifted into Chinatown, just a block away. Shortly after 9 P.M. someone pitched a rock through a window. The crowd erupted. Sticks, stones, bricks, and bottles filled the air as the mob rampaged through Chinatown to break every store window.

The residents of Chinatown were terrified. "We lived in Shanghai Alley," recalls Lillian Ho Wong, who was a youngster of twelve then.

Shanghai Alley, after the riot. The broken windows were boarded up. Notice the plants and laundry of the upper storey living quarters. The Chinese sign at the far left pointed to the "Theatre Upstairs."

A 1907 view of the 400-block Carrall Street showing the Sam Kee Company storefront and, at the corner, the Methodist Chinese Mission.

Merchant Chang Toy of the Sam Kee Company.

''One store had lights on, and all the glass there was shattered. Papa came back and said, 'Don't put on the lights! And don't sit near the windows!' They were running through all the lanes, making all kinds of noise. We had no lights on, so they couldn't see us. We sat in the centre, so that if anything happened at either end, we could still run out.''

The destruction only lasted five minutes. Then the rioters headed towards Japantown. When they returned, it took the police four hours to control them.

Next day, white crowds tried several times to invade Chinatown, but the area was roped off and guarded by police. The Chinese carried rocks, bottles, and bricks to the tops of their buildings to hurl at the rioters if they came through again. On Monday

After the riot, at Fongoun's, 1907. This store, at 100 East Hastings Street, had a manager, a bookkeeper, three coatmakers earning forty-five dollars a month, two ladies' tailors earning fifty dollars a month, and four tailors sewing pants and vests who earned thirty-five dollars a month.

The Canadian Pacific Railway Chinese
Agent Yip Sang.

Merchant Yip Sang and family members in
front of his store, c. 1902. Yip had enlarged
the original two-storey building (dated 1889
in the photo) by adding more street
frontage, the bay-windowed second storey,
and an entire third floor in 1901.

morning, the Chinese hurried
to arm themselves.

"We could have sold every
gun in the store," said a
salesman at McLennan,
McFeely and Company. "As
soon as we opened there was a
steady stream of Chinese in
search of revolvers. And no
cheap guns, either, for the
Chinese buy better guns than
the average white man. This
morning the cheapest gun we
sold at $15, and one Chinaman

ordered fifteen at $20.50 each.
I daresay we must have sold
over a hundred before the
police asked us to shut down
on the sale."

The Chinese held a general
strike in the city for three days.
Hundreds of Chinese left their
jobs. Downtown hotels and
restaurants, West End homes,
steamers, logging camps, and
shingle mills were all suddenly
inconvenienced. And several
major Chinese landowners

employed a small army of
watchmen to guard their
property against attacks.

In May of 1908 William Lyon
Mackenzie King, then deputy
minister of labour, conducted
hearings into the riot in
Vancouver. He awarded the
merchants of Chinatown
$3,185 for property damage
(mostly broken windows) and
$20,236 for business losses
suffered in the days following
the riot.

The Merchant Princes

The reporters for
Vancouver's English-language
newspapers marvelled at the
astounding wealth of Chinatown's merchant princes when
they testified before William
Lyon Mackenzie King's investi-
gation of the 1907 riot.
According to the *Province*:

*This morning the two
wealthiest celestials in British
Columbia appeared, Loo Gee
Wing and Sam Kee, their*

combined wealth exceeding a million dollars. Their spectacular appearance was followed by two lonely looking wives of absent Chinamen. Sam Kee has property holdings in Chinatown worth half a million, paying an annual tax to the city of over $3000.

This was the remarkable difference between Loo and Sam: the former dressed like a tailor's model in the suit of a prosperous Englishman down to his patent leathers, while Sam still retains his Chinese costume and speaks only in his native tongue.

Sam Kee was actually the name of the firm founded by Chang Toy, but the company and its white customers all called him Sam Kee. In Chinatown, Sam Kee contracted labour for shingle mills and canneries, handled imported Chinese foodstuffs, and sold steamship tickets for the Blue Funnel Line. The company also exported salt herring and manufactured charcoal.

Meanwhile, back at Mackenzie King's inquiry, the reporter saw that another pioneer businessman had arrived:

"Did you lose any export orders during the week of the riot?" the commissioner asked Yip Sang, who supplies the Empress liners with the food required for Chinese crews, and as the head of the Wing Sang Company Limited, does an importing and exporting trade of $50,000 a year.

"No," replied the merchant prince of Chinatown, "the riot did not affect us that way. Our stores and houses were damaged to the extent of $450 and we lost about $100 in local trade."

Questioned as to the value of the property owned by the

eight merchant tailors because of the great Canadian dilemma over freight rates. Vancouver wholesalers preferred local goods because the costs of shipping from the east reduced their profits, so they contracted out job orders to Chinese merchant tailors.[8] Over one hundred Chinese worked for merchant tailors, making boys' wear and workmen's clothing. Custom tailors produced made-to-measure suits for white clients, and by 1907 there were even three shops, conveniently located away from the heart of Chinatown, producing fancy silk goods for white women.

Chinatown was regularly denounced as unclean and disease-ridden by city officials. The medical health officer was also concerned with overcrowded tenements, lack of ventilation, and cellar lodgings in Chinatown.[9] The shores of False Creek were used as dumping grounds for human wastes and garbage until Chinatown was finally connected to a sewer in 1896. That same year, city officials destroyed four rows of shacks built over the foreshore and filled the site to street level.

Between 1900 and 1910 a building boom gripped Chinatown as Chinese merchants bought land and erected their own buildings. Mortgages came from mainstream trust companies and white businessmen. The buildings were made of brick, usually three storeys high, and often with an extra cheater floor between the main and second floors. They resembled town buildings of south China with recessed balconies and decorative wrought-metal railings. Storefronts on the main floor faced both street and alley. Market Alley, running between Pender and Hastings streets, thrived with barbers, bakeries, and laundries, while the buildings facing Carrall Street opened onto Shanghai Alley. The upper floors of buildings were used as residences, boarding houses, and meeting halls. Chinatown was densely populated indeed.

Page from a Chinese-English phrasebook, published in Vancouver in 1910. For each English sentence, there are two lines of Chinese, one giving a literal translation and one teaching pronunciation of the English. From *Chinese-English Phrasebook* (Vancouver: Thomson Stationery Company, 1897)

company and chiefly by Yip Sang, he estimated it at $200,000.

"We own a full half interest in all the land and buildings in Canton Street, eight stores on Dupont Street, four stores and four houses on Carrall Street, and three stores on Hastings Street."

Like his competitor Chang Toy, Yip Sang had risen from poverty-stricken origins to the top of Chinatown's financial mountain. Yip, for example, landed penniless in San Francisco and panned for gold, cooked, washed dishes, and worked in a cigar factory. In 1881 he trekked north to the Cariboo, wheeling his few belongings along in a cart. Failing to find his fortune there, he headed south and became a foreman for a Chinese labour contractor on the Canadian Pacific Railway. When the railroad was built,

The receiving room of the Lee Yune Company, c. 1895. At the right is co-manager Lee Sai-fan; with him are his cousin and brother. The firm legally imported and manufactured opium.

36   The Merchants

Chinatown's most notable citizens were its successful merchants. Yip Sang of Wing Sang Company, Chang Toy of Sam Kee Company, partners Leong Suey and Lum Duck Shew of Gim Lee Yuen, Wong Soon King of Hip Tuck Lung, and Lee Kee of Lee Yuen were the wealthiest men of Chinatown. In 1907 the latter four firms reported gross incomes of $150,000 to $180,000 annually.[10] They prospered in import-export trade, labour contracting, and real estate. Lee Yuen and Hip Tuck Lung processed opium, then a legal and very lucrative enterprise.

Land was the most prized of assets, and the merchants invested heavily in it. For example, Yip Sang headed a Chinese syndicate that built the apartment block and tenement complex known as Canton Alley. Chang Toy owned ten lots in Chinatown, two corner sites in Gastown, at least five hotels downtown, water frontage on the south shore of False Creek, and land in southeast Vancouver, Burnaby, North

Man Lee Company advertisement, 1901.

Mark Long Ltd. advertisement, 1901.

Yip won the position of Chinese agent for the CPR, handling its lucrative Chinese passenger and freight business.

Also appearing before Mackenzie King was the firm of Hip Tuck Lung, a licensed opium manufacturer that had a staff of nineteen and earned a gross income of $170,000 in 1907. Another merchant, partner Leong Suey of the Gim Lee Yuen Company, testified

that he had started thirteen stores and that his two current operations brought him an annual business of $150,000.[16]

The Last of the Giants

The September 1911 issue of *B.C. Magazine* carried this lively account of the Chinese workers who cleared the land for the new city of Vancouver.

A gang of expert Chinese will clean a lot in less time than a gang of any other nationality. That is one reason why Chinese of the coolie class should be welcome in this country. All a land clearer needs is a calloused skin and a

dumb philosophy which refuses to recognize weariness and forgets man's right to pursue happiness. Brains are unnecessary, but as in all cases, they help. That is why the Chinese coolie, whose brain is of infinitesimal proportions, is preferable....

Fong has a subtler method. First he digs a hole down among the roots and running inward with a slant, so that the bottom of the shaft is under

Chinese land clearer at work. From *B.C. Magazine,* September 1911.

the centre of the stump. Then he drops in three or four packages of oiled paper containing a black powder. The last package has a white fuse fastened to it. He tamps the charge with sand and packs it well. About this time the gang starts for distant points of safety, warning back rigs and people on the road. Fong touches a live coal to the fuse and sprints away, yelling as he goes. Swiftly the charge does its work, striking upward with smashing force, splitting the solid trunk from base to summit like an apple, and sending the roar of its thunder across the fields. The gang come[s] back like a flock of dirty bluebirds. They grab the broken stump with their peavies, roll it over to the fast-growing heap and set the whole on fire.

All day the fight goes on. The blue smoke of the fires hangs lazily over the field, and the Chinese move about in its clinging wreaths like soldiers in the dust of a battle. They have their axes, peavies, spades, blasting powder and a trifling intelligence, which they pit against the stubborn resistance of the last of the giants. The Chinese win in the end. When at length they gather up their shoulder poles and baskets, . . . the field is level as a lawn.[17]

A Carrall Street merchant tailor store, 1898. These small factories supplied ready-made clothing to department stores, which in turn sold to the city's growing population.

W. H. Chow (building contractor)
advertisement, 1908. From *Henderson's
Directory*

Sam Kee Company invoice.

Vancouver, Steveston, and Caulfeild, as
well as the Hastings Townsite.[11]

One remarkable characteristic of
the merchants was their outspokenness
with city hall. In petitions throughout
the 1890s that they submitted either
themselves or through white lawyers,
they campaigned for improved
sidewalks and services to their
community. They formed the Chinese
Board of Trade in 1895 to promote trade
and to protect the local Chinese. At
about the same time, the Chinese
Benevolent Association was established
to unify the community, settle internal
disputes, help the sick and poor, and
defend the community against external
threats.

Only merchants could afford to
bring their wives over, and those who
came were often secondary wives
because first wives were left at home to
manage family affairs. In China it was
socially acceptable and status-
enhancing to have more than one wife.
The first wife retained primacy and
authority in the family; the second was

acquired to produce additional male
heirs. Although the terms were used
interchangeably by Westerners,
secondary wives were not concubines,
who had no reproductive duties and
were not officially married.[12]

In accordance with Chinese tradition, adult women were rarely seen on
the streets. In the Chinese theatre, a
separate seating section was set aside for
them. Their children attended Central
School, located just west of Chinatown,
for a standard English education. At
home, private tutors might be brought
in to teach Chinese. On Sundays some
children attended church at the Chinese
Methodist Mission. The children's dress
was Western, and they wore traditional
Chinese garments only for special
events such as photograph sessions or
the Chinese New Year.

The Common Folk

The merchants stood out as local
success stories, as Old Country fellows
who had made good. They had stores,
homes, and families to show. But for the

The Revolution Comes to Town

By the time Dr. Sun Yat-sen
visited Vancouver in 1910 and
1911, he had lived the colourful
and dangerous life of a hunted
revolutionary. He had
engineered nine armed
uprisings to try to seize power,
and was later revered as the
father of modern China. In the
overseas Chinese
communities, not all Chinese
agreed with Dr. Sun's revolutionary rhetoric. Still, he held a
special appeal to them because
he was born in the Pearl River
delta area from which most
North American immigrants
had come.

Chang Yun Ho was born in
1887 and came to Canada
when he was twenty-one. He
recalls hearing the famous
leader speak in Vancouver:

*He spoke the same dialect I
do, and so he spoke
Cantonese with a Shek-ki*

Dr. Sun Yat-sen, the "Father of Modern
China." This photo was taken by Vancouver
photographer Yucho Chow in 1911 when
the revolutionary leader was in Vancouver.

Mrs. Jin Chong Ho, c. 1900. She came to Canada in 1888 at the age of fifteen. Lillian Ho recalled that her mother always wore Western clothing.

vast majority of Chinatown's men, their wives and families waited back in China. A worker trapped in seasonal and transient jobs could hardly settle in one place to raise a family, especially with the expensive head taxes levied on Chinese people entering Canada. And blatant anti-Chinese hostility was no encouragement to bring over a family. A man could send money and letters home, and then turn to prostitutes, gambling, and opium for solace. The early Christian missions tried to steer the men away from these diversions and offered them night school English classes.

The church was one of the few Canadian institutions that reached out to the Chinese. It wanted to win heathen souls for Christ, better the immigrants' social lot, and improve interracial relations. Church work among the Chinese had begun in 1888 when the Methodist Mission set up night classes near Chinatown. Eleven Chinese were baptized in August, but the number of converts grew very slowly. In 1895 the

The Chinese Freemasons' Building on the northwest corner of Pender and Carrall, 1911. Dr. Sun Yat-sen allegedly stayed here during his visits to Vancouver.

accent. Most people here were from Say-yup and they didn't understand him. They said if Dr. Sun couldn't make them understand his speech, how was he going to get China back from the Manchus?

They were swearing in the background while he was talking. His talk lasted for two or three hours. Then he asked for suggestions and people asked him questions about his plans. He answered in a very

calm, confident tone. Some people contributed money on the spot. I did too, and Dr. Sun wrote out a receipt to each person who contributed.

But there was a difference of opinion among people here. Those people from Chung-shan were very enthusiastic about supporting him, but Say-yup people were doubtful, and they would ask embarrassing questions like, "You don't even have a ship or

Yip Sang family members, 1906. A corresponding photo of Yip Sang with all the *males* of the family was also taken. He had twenty-three children: nineteen sons and four daughters.

a gun, how are you going to
overthrow a whole dynasty?"
And "You don't have any
money, all you have is talk."

Many of the people who
were against him were for the
Chinese Empire Reform
Association. And there were
skirmishes between the two
groups. [18]

Chinatown Children
Childhood in early
Chinatown was an experience
far different from that of other
Vancouver children. Born here
in 1895, Lillian Ho Wong
discovered opium to be as
common as chores and
punishment:

Uncle Opium Kwun-jong
lived upstairs and he smoked
opium. Sometimes I would
leave my baby sister with him
and run off to play. Mama

found out and she spanked
me, saying, "Those opium
ghosts, what do they know
about taking care of children?
Those opium ghosts, they
don't think. They can't even
take care of themselves! What
if they burn my baby?"

Uncle Opium Kwun-jong
had a special lamp for heating
the opium and special scissors
to cut the wick. You heated the
opium until it bubbled up, then
you put it on the pipe. So one

day when he went out, I lit the
lamp and cut the opium and
heated it. It had a very sweet
smell. But I cut it all wrong, so
he knew I had been fiddling. I
got spanked.

He would scrape the opium
soot off the pipe and boil it
with potatoes, mash it and roll
it into pills and carry them
around in his pocket. Just like
snuff. I saw that, but I didn't
understand it and I went and
scraped off all his pipes. I told

Rev. Hugh P. Hobson, Baptist missionary
and first rector of Christ Church Cathedral,
with a group of Chinese converts, c. 1895.

Presbyterian Church opened its mission in Chinatown to offer English classes and the gospel too.

The women of Chinatown were maidservants or prostitutes, if they were not the wives and daughters of merchants. Maidservants were girls who had been sold by their parents as domestic help. Their new families provided them with food, clothing, and shelter, as well as kinship status as secondary daughters. Owners also found the girl a husband when she reached marrying age so that she might establish her own family and life.[13]

Old World Politics

If money and families were not available to all, Old World politics was, although it naturally created divisions. In the 1890s people in Chinatowns around the world followed the international power struggles of China with great interest. In 1895 the Chinese were stunned when China's navy was destroyed by Japan in battle. Calls to modernize and strengthen China's

45

him, "I've just cleaned all your pipes, Uncle!" and got spanked again.

Outdoor play was limited to the streets and open areas nearby. As Dick Yip remembers:

Most of the time we played outside at the railroad tracks. There was not much room to play so we played around the cars, under the boxcars. It was dangerous but we didn't know. Sometimes we played in False

Creek, in the water. We were afraid to go out of Chinese territory. I didn't go to the park until I was older.

For other children, childhood meant nothing but work. The wealthy merchants brought over young girls to work as maidservants. Some girls were mistreated, and this prompted the Methodist Women's Missionary Society to open a Rescue Home in Victoria for runaway girls and

prostitutes in the late 1880s. Elsie Hong Yet became a maidservant in 1900 at age seven:

Yip Yen's family brought me over, but they gave me to Yip Yen's brother's second wife. She wouldn't let me go to school; all the other servant girls in Yip Sang's household went to school. She worked me all day long. I got up at seven in the morning to light the stove in the room. They

would still be sleeping. The stove burned coal, so I had to rake out the ashes. Of course that made noise, and she would scold me for waking her.

When she got up, I made her toast and tea and coffee. Then I washed the dishes. I cooked the rice, I scrubbed the clothes and the floors. After she ate her fill at dinner, she'd go out to play dominoes with the Jung Kee lady and leave me working. There used to be

seamsters in Chinatown, and she brought home clothing for me to work on: feather-stitching, buttonholes, butterfly buttons—I did everything. I worked from morning until night without stopping.

When I was about eight or nine, I hurt my foot. Dr. Munro wanted to cut it off, but they said, "Don't! Who will want a wife without a leg? Just let her be! If she lives, she lives."

Christianity Creates Canadians

The swiftest cultural transformations from Chinese to Canadian ways of life occurred among immigrants who converted to Christianity.

Fong Dickman came to Canada in 1884 at age twenty-four and drove a stagecoach. He studied English at the first Methodist Mission that opened in Vancouver's Chinatown in 1888 and was made a

missionary in 1898. His daughter Anna Fong Lam reports: "Father used to go down and preach in the street with a portable organ. I don't know who played for him, but he used to take it down and sing hymns and preach in the street. He had night classes with over a hundred young men coming to learn English. I would say quite a number of them became Christians."

Armed with a new Western

perspective, Chinese-Canadian missionaries often condemned the "backward" ways of their fellow countrymen. Methodist preacher Tom Chu Thom:

The chief sin of our race in this country is to set up a monument of Chinatown wherever they go—a bad example, with gambling and opium smoking. They set up the different tongues to quarrelling and fighting amongst themselves. They

political and military machines arose. But reform efforts led by scholars Kang You-wei and Liang Qi-chao were crushed by the Empress Dowager, and they fled into exile. The two scholar-reformers visited Vancouver several times seeking funds to support their movement. In 1899 Kang established a branch of his Chinese Empire Reform Association in Vancouver and received support from established merchants for his proposal to modernize China with a constitutional monarchy based on a Confucian model of government.

Dr. Sun Yat-sen, on the other hand, cried out for an armed revolution in China. He wanted to overthrow the monarchy and set up a new republic based on nationalism, democracy, and social well-being. In Canada, Dr. Sun won the support of the Chinese Freemasons, originally known as the Chi Kung Tong, a traditional fraternal organization that originated in China. Members mortgaged their buildings to raise funds for him. In Vancouver, a newspaper debate heated up because both the Chinese Empire Reform Association and the Freemasons had their own newspapers.

Saltwater City's Chinese were keen to see a stronger China partly because Canada continued to treat them shabbily. In 1902 the head tax rose to one hundred dollars; a year later it went up to five hundred dollars. Provincial laws had been passed forbidding the Chinese to vote, or to own or work on Crown lands. Because they were not allowed on the provincial voters' list, later generations of Chinese Canadians could not enter certain professions such as accountancy, law, and pharmacy. In Vancouver, Chinese could not be employed on city contracts. The local Chinese were powerless to stop such laws. But they thought that if China were stronger, then perhaps fairer treatment might be accorded them.

In 1911 the revolution succeeded and imperial China was finished forever. By then Chinatown had become a substantial community. Some of its men had made fortunes in the classic rags-to-riches rise and brought their families over for a fresh start in the New World. These men became symbols of hope to the hundreds of Chinese who remained trapped in low-paying jobs. And white Canada was not totally closed to the Chinese: the Christian churches reached out to them, the Chinese could borrow money from whites, and new immigrants could open their own shops for a chance at quick profits. Furthermore, dramatic events in their homeland gave Chinese here hope that the old ways would not last forever.

import slave girls to sell for prostitution. They love their dead friends more than their live ones. They worship at the graveyard three times a year. They ride steam engines and locomotive cars every day in this country, but most of them believe in mountain, wind, and water gods. . . . By observation they ought to know better.[19]

Still, Thom believed Christianity brought practical benefits for the Chinese: "The money-makers in Chinatown don't want to see the Chinese get converted because they can't cheat them as easily as the unconverted ones."

The Chinese-Canadian missionaries themselves provided shining examples of the assimilability of the immigrants. Reverend Fong Dickman's wife Jane Cheng had been educated in an English boarding school and could read and write Chinese and English, as well as play the piano. Her daughter Anna Lam recalls, "My father read a lot and we were encouraged to read, too. Mother used to send away to England for books and magazines for us. And we were voracious readers. She got the Arthur Mead books, which were children's books. They tried to teach us Chinese at home, but it didn't sink in."

Rev. Fong Dickman with his family at the Chinese Methodist Mission, c. 1905.

The United Christian Society (Methodist) picnic at Stanley Park, Dominion Day, 1912. Reverends Yiu-tan Chan, Fong Dickman and Joh-yuen Lim gather by the portable organ.

Chinese Canadians: The Community Grows

The year 1911 saw the start of a new China, and 1923 marked the end of Chinese immigration to Canada. In the intervening years, Saltwater City's Chinese population grew from thirty-five hundred to sixty-five hundred. More women arrived: in 1911 there were twenty-eight Chinese men for every one Chinese female; that ratio dropped to ten-to-one for Vancouver by 1921.[1] Vancouver had 210 Chinese families in 1919, and Canadian-borns formed 7 per cent of the community.[2] Chinatown pushed beyond the Pender-Carrall area into Strathcona, and the Chinese also moved outside their home territory as Vancouver's growing population encouraged small businesses to settle in new neighbourhoods.[3]

The city's rapid growth had been fuelled by Canada's rush to populate the prairies, which spawned a house-building boom that peaked in 1912. Demand for British Columbia lumber plummeted after that and left a severe recession in its place. Not until 1916 did wartime demands for B.C.'s raw materials and ships briefly revitalize the city's economy.

By then 80 per cent of Vancouver's Chinese were estimated to be jobless, so many who could raise passage headed back to China. Because of the disruption of shipping during World War I, they were allowed to stay there until one year after the declaration of peace. Joblessness in Chinatown was further aggravated by high prices and shortages of imported foods such as rice. In response, a co-operative store called the United Chinese Provision and Supply Company started in Vancouver, issuing shares at twenty-five cents each.[4]

Immigration dropped too: between 1915 and 1918, only 1,250 Chinese came in, compared to the 7,445 who had arrived during the single fiscal year of 1912-13. In December of 1913 the Chinese Benevolent Association (CBA) of Victoria requested officials in Guangdong province to stop people from coming to Canada because of the joblessness.[5]

In January of 1915 the *ad hoc* Vancouver Chinese Salvation and Welfare Committee started serving free meals to destitute men at the CBA. Musicians from the local Chinese theatre raised funds with a benefit concert. This canteen service lasted until summer but reopened in January of 1916 to distribute rice, while another group, the Vancouver Chinese United Association, served meals. The free distribution of food stopped again in May when summer work became available at farms and canneries.[6]

Racism

White racism was part of everyday life for Saltwater City's Chinese people. Their movements to and from Canada were rigorously monitored. They had no voting rights and found only low-paying jobs in a few sectors of the economy. Even when they worked, there was trouble. City hall levied high fees on

Cover from novel *The Writing on the Wall,*
1923.

Chinese pedlars in 1915, tried to fire hotel workers in 1916, and fined grocers over hygiene rules in 1917.[7] When added to the continual police raids on gambling, drugs, and liquor in Chinatown, all these actions revealed the severity of white opposition.

Some Chinese felt there was no justice in Canada. Newspapers reported that white boys who stoned a Chinese girl had escaped punishment and that a presiding judge defended a hit-and-run driver who had killed a Chinese.[8] When the Chinese applied for citizenship, they were often refused. Judge Grant of the County Court routinely rejected Chinese applicants who came before him.

"Do you think the country is strengthened and made better by adding a hundred thousand of this man's race to the Lower Mainland?" the judge asked when Mr. Yew Gan Hoy appeared before him. "When I die I want to leave a country a fit place for my children to live in. My duty is not to report any person whom I don't believe would *make this country better or keep it as good as it is."[9]*

In the late 1910s two powerful campaigns were mounted against the Chinese. One came from white farmers of the province, who wanted to prevent Chinese from owning or leasing farmland. Delegates from the province's Farmers' Institutes testified before the Agriculture Committee of the Legislature:

The Orientals have control of the markets in Vancouver and other cities. Many of them are cooks. If you do not let them do their buying of potatoes, for instance, they say the potatoes are no good and they cook them so they are no good. Then they say, if you let us buy, we will get good potatoes. They go and get them from Orientals and in this way the whole market is being controlled by them. Once they have got the land, look out, there the mischief starts. We have nothing to fear in passing laws against them. They can't retaliate.[10]

The other outcry came from storekeepers protesting the movement of

Getting Here

Before the gates of exclusion slammed shut on 1 July 1923, the coming-over stories of the "bachelor" men and boys were poignant tales that became legendary for later generations of their families. The first step away from the village led to Hong Kong. Harry Chin, who left China in 1920 when he was fourteen, tells how his trip started:

There were two men

Harry Chin and his friend Sing Tai Chin, shortly after arriving in Vancouver, 1921.

returning to Canada from my village so they brought me along. In Hong Kong we stayed at a "Gold Mountain shop," which boarded passengers for the ships. My classmate Sing-tai was also going to Vancouver, so we ran all around. We took the electric tram to the top of Tai Ping Mountain, then we went to see an opera. When we went back to the shop at night, the two men returning to Canada *thought we had been kidnapped!"*

At the docks of Hong Kong, authorities checked the immigrants' belongings and fumigated them with foul-smelling sulphur. Wong Quan was nineteen when he boarded the Blue Goose in 1918:

My father saw me off at the boat. Just my father came because it was so expensive to travel in those days. He didn't want me to leave him. I didn't

Wong Lee Company truck, c. 1920. Delivery trucks such as these were seen throughout Vancouver. "Everyone got to eat, after all."

Chinese grocers into white neighbourhoods and the longer working hours that they put in. Both these campaigns shrilly warned that Asians would soon control the British Columbia economy. Storekeepers garnered support from the Retail Merchants Association, the Vancouver Board of Trade, and newspapers, one of which editorialized as follows:

Every man and woman in this province can make himself or herself into an Asiatic Exclusion League by the simple method of patronizing white merchants and white laundries and white workers, whenever possible. It may involve a little mutual sacrifice all around, but it is a sacrifice that will pay. The man who saves 60 cents a week on his grocery bill by buying from a Chinese grocer is a loser for he is helping to undermine his own job.[11]

Anti-Chinese news made good copy for newspapers, and the *Vancouver Daily World* sensationalized the drug connection, warning that "little tawdry white girls [were] taken round in

want to leave him. We cried. He gave me three dollars for spending money. There was a same-villager returning to Canada on the same boat. We hadn't even been going for half an hour when he came to ask for money. So I lent him my three dollars, he went and gambled it away, and I never got it back.

The voyage across the Pacific took one month. When the ship reached Japan to take

on coal, the Chinese passengers had to strip, line up in two lines, and let a Japanese doctor inspect them. Japanese vendors came aboard to sell foods and toys, but patriotic Chinese resented Japan's incursions into China and refused to buy from them.

For the rest of the voyage the passengers slept, ate, and gambled to pass the time. The meals covered by the passage fee were badly prepared,

according to Jung Hong Len who travelled in 1912 aboard the *Empress of India*:

There was fish and all kinds of things, but it wasn't cooked very well. The ship hands didn't want you to eat your fill, because they wanted you to buy the other food they were selling. They made sausage rice, salty-egg rice, and pressed-duck rice for twenty cents a bowl.

For breakfast they sold rice

congee *and* bahk-gwoh *(gingko nut) congee for the people who felt the boat was hot and stuffy. As soon as the eating was finished, they opened tables for gambling:* fan-tan, pai-gow, *everything. If you didn't gamble, you slept. If you weren't seasick, you could visit around the ship. If you were seasick, you slept.*

When the ship finally docked in Vancouver, a stony welcome awaited arrivals at

December 1, 1921   10c

Danger: The Anti-Asiatic Weekly, 1921.

curtained taxis to the Chinese labor camps and lodging houses so that they might use the money to purchase more of the evil stuff."[12] In 1921 the Sun Publishing Company released a lurid novel that suggested the Chinese could spread typhoid and the plague among the white population through their control of the food supply.[13] That same year, another Vancouver Asiatic Exclusion League was formed, and its goal was to end Asian immigration into Canada.

Between 1919 and 1922 another recession hit the economy when peacetime reduced war production and workers' wages. Chinese jobs were lost and wages dropped: a cook's salary fell from ninety dollars a month to fifty dollars.[14] Thousands of soldiers returned to Canada and found no work, so veterans' organizations and trade unions railed against the Chinese, accusing them of taking jobs that rightfully belonged to whites. In January 1921, when Vancouver's Chinese joined white church groups for a tag day to raise

money for famine relief in China, unemployed veterans picketed the young canvassers with signs reading, "Canada first—China last," and "Why not take care of our own homeless, starving, and unemployed?"[15]

The issue of school segregation emerged too. The only Chinese students who were segregated were those who attended schools with large Chinese enrolments and who had a poor command of English. But in 1920 the Children's Protective Association called for removing Chinese students from the classroom altogether. It complained that the older Chinese students posed a moral threat to younger students and slowed the class's progress in school work. There were 490 Chinese in the elementary schools in 1921—of whom 45 were over the age of sixteen—and 33 Chinese in the high schools.[16]

To forestall segregation, the Chinese Benevolent Association (CBA) and the Chinese consul met with the Chinese students and instructed them to obey all rules, keep clean, and make

Quon On Jan Travel Agency, 1915. It competed against Wing Sang Company, agent for the Canadian Pacific Railway Company. The CPR had both railway and steamships, so Canadian National teamed with the Blue Funnel Line to provide quick land-ocean travel back to China.

the immigration station on the waterfront at the north end of Burrard Street. Immigrants have few fond memories of their enforced stay there while officials checked their papers and their health. Jack Lee came in 1921 at the age of eight and was kept in the station for three months:

We were like prisoners. There were bars in the windows. There was roll call, bed call, a time to sleep, a time

Students and staff of the Mon Wah School at their Christmas exhibition of student work, 1925. This was one of five Chinese-language schools in Chinatown at that time.

good impressions in the classroom. The CBA even hired a dentist to examine the teeth of all Chinese students prior to the start of school.[17] But total segregation was never implemented because Vancouver's school principals dismissed charges that Asians hindered class progress.[18] In Victoria, however, all Chinese students were removed to a separate school in 1922, and this sparked an enormous protest from both the Vancouver and Victoria Chinese.

Because of this ground swell of anti-Chinese feeling, B.C. politicians moved to pressure the federal Parliament into stopping Chinese immigration. On 1 July 1923, a new Chinese Immigration Act came into effect. Only four kinds of Chinese immigrants were allowed: diplomats, children born in Canada, students, and merchants. During the next twenty-four years, only forty-four Chinese people entered. Thereafter, Chinese Canadians called the first of July Humiliation Day and refused to join Dominion Day activities.

Head Tax Certificate, 1921.

to wake up, just like in the army camp. The Chinese called it "the piglet pen." There were guards to keep you in line: you couldn't go outside the compound without permission, and visitors were regulated.

The food was very bad: generally there was a dish of soup, then they used the same meat from the soup and mixed it with vegetables and served it with rice. That was supposed to be Chinese food. The station was noisy too, with trains going back and forth all day long. The five-hundred-dollar head tax? It would be equal to fifteen thousand dollars today![28]

Lion dance, possibly for Chinese Freemasons' celebration, at Pender and Carrall, c. 1920.

Local Chinese rallied with protests against this hostile landslide of restrictive laws and government lobbying. Vegetable pedlars and laundrymen engaged legal help to fight their cases before the courts.[19] Student clubs and theatre groups raised funds to counterlobby the governments.[20] But Chinese Canadians were powerless without the vote and their numbers were small. Although they organized solid support within their community, they could do little, for example, to influence the 1923 immigration act.

Still, they did derive small satisfaction from their efforts. They read in their newspapers of how Chinese car-washers for the Great Northern Railway had been replaced by war veterans, only to have the ex-soldiers go on strike when wages were reduced. The Chinese Freemasons' lawyers successfully charged a white man with assaulting a Chinese ironworker who even received financial compensation. The value of protest was never lost, because sometimes it paid off. In 1921, after repeated complaints from Mrs. Nellie Yip, Vancouver General Hospital dropped its discriminatory policy of diverting all Chinese patients to the basement.[21]

Community Organizations

Men who were suddenly thrust into the New World faced staggering problems. They had to find work and shelter in a world where a different language was spoken, where jobs were limited, and where the competition for work was fierce. An individual's clan name and home district provided an easy basis for making contacts and friends, so prominent organizations grew from these points of commonality. Men united to help one another because ultimately the greater good (that is, the lineage back home) would be better served if everyone did well over here.

By 1923 Vancouver had twenty-six clan associations and twelve Old Country home-district organizations. Their size and wealth varied: the Wongs, Lees, and Chans were among

---

Working As a Houseboy

For many Chinese immigrants, a common first job was houseboy service. Almost every well-to-do white family in town had one. The hard work and eagerness of these servants endeared them to employers, but the workers' view was different. Wing Wong arrived in Vancouver in 1912 and went to work as a houseboy. Wong Quan arrived in 1918.

WING WONG: *The discrimination was so bad you couldn't get any other work except housework. That was forced, you had to do housework because you went into the house and nobody saw you. That way, people didn't mind. But if you went into the public and looked for work, you sure got beat up.*

I was small in those days, twelve or thirteen. I studied after school and then I did my work: *chopping wood, bringing up coal, house-cleaning, taking care of the furnace, washing dishes. Just to get my room and board.*
WONG QUAN: *I washed the dishes, and the lady of the house taught me to fry bacon and eggs and to make toast on the stove. I lived downstairs, near the coal in the basement. I slept on an old broken bed. I broke coal into smaller pieces, washed the car, washed the* dog. *Mrs. Johnson treated me well. She made the salad, and we all ate together.*

At the second place, on Fifteenth Avenue near Kingsway, the lady had two sons who were very bad. At night, when I was asleep, they came down with sheets around them like ghosts to pick on me. When I burned the coal and it was not warm enough, they scolded me. I bought an orange to eat and

Yip Gong and his wife Nellie were one of Vancouver's first interracial couples. Yip, a jeweller, brought Nellie from New York to live in the Yip family building. Nellie, who worked as a midwife and translator in Chinatown, spoke five Chinese dialects fluently.

they stole it. The boys were so bad that I quit after a few months.

In 1914 a Chinese houseboy was involved in a sensational murder story. Wing Wong recalls, ''This lady was murdered and the houseboy was accused. Her body was taken to the cellar and cut up in pieces and burnt in the furnace. From then on, oh boy, was it bad! No Chinese could walk on the street without being stoned.''

The accused, sixteen-year-old Jack Kong, had worked for the Charles Millards in their West End home. When the police confronted him with damning evidence, he quickly confessed. He said Mrs. Millard had scolded him on the morning of 1 April for burning the breakfast porridge and ordered him to cook some more. Kong had refused because he would be late for

Newspaper sketch of houseboy Jack Kong. From the Millard murder story in *Daily Province*, 21 May 1914

One aspect of the solidarity of the Chinese family is revealed in the photograph (facing page) taken in Zhongshan, China, c. 1915. In the middle row, far right, is Lee Dye, a prominent merchant of Victoria. Seated next to him is his father. The man in the back row is Lee Dye's son, George Kun Lee, also known as Lee Teenjore, a herbalist in Vancouver. A close look reveals that Lee Dye's image is the earlier photograph (this page), which has been added onto the family photo.

the most numerous in Vancouver, as were people from the four counties of Say-yup. Large clans erected substantial buildings in Chinatown containing dormitories, commercial rental space, and meeting halls; smaller clans bought houses nearby. Association leaders provided work in their stores or through the labour contracts that they handled. There were also social activities such as reading rooms and New Year's banquets for members. In China, powerful lineages gave prestige to their members; here, wealthy clan and district organizations provided pride and a sense of well-being for displaced migrants.

Direct links with China were maintained, too. Associations sent cash remittances and the bones of deceased members home. They tried to improve conditions at home by raising money to build modern high schools there. They collected funds for bandit victims because returnees from Canada and their families were often targets for robbery or kidnapping. They raised

school. He said she seized the bread knife and threatened to cut off his ear. He grabbed a chair to defend himself and when she lunged at him, he brought it down on her head and she dropped dead. He then tried to dispose of the body.

When Kong appeared in court, extra police were called in. A *Province* reporter noted, "It was by all odds the largest throng that ever attempted to gain admittance to a Vancouver police court." Fashionably dressed West End and Shaughnessy matrons, working women, and shopgirls "scrambled and fought their way up the two flights of stairs." They brought lunches wrapped in tissue paper to make a day of the event. It was as if the darkest fears about the Chinese had come true. Trusting families had taken houseboys into their homes, and here one boy had suddenly turned on the woman of the house. Some fearful families reportedly discharged their houseboys.

The prosecution alleged Kong had stabbed Mrs. Millard and was using the chair story as a cover-up. The defence countered that Kong had no motive for murder and had better chances to kill her without leaving such a trail of evidence. The jury had to decide if Kong was guilty of murder or manslaughter, or innocent of all criminal intent by way of justifiable homicide. The jury returned a verdict of guilty of manslaughter, and Kong was sentenced to life imprisonment. Seven years later, he was deported to China.[29]

Kwong Yee Lung Company truck parked at 837 Keefer Street, c. 1920. The company handled Chinese herbs. Earnest Yet, an avid amateur photographer, took this picture. His wife Elsie stands to the far left.

Working Door to Door

Vivid and fond were the memories that Vancouverites held of the Chinese who came to their doors. "We had the Chinese laundryman who took the washing each week," city archivist J. S. Matthews recalled in 1945. "We bought vegetables from the Chinaman at the back door, and fish from the Chinaman who carried it in two buckets at the ends of a shoulder pole. The wooden lid he turned over and used as a chopping block after we had decided which fish we wanted. Nice fresh fish, too."

Vegetable pedlars had long been seen on Vancouver streets. Their horse-carts and trucks brought fresh fruits and vegetables to householders regularly because modern refrigeration was lacking in most homes. But white store-keepers resented these Chinese competitors. An 1894 civic bylaw limited the sale of fresh food products to "permanent" places of business, and Chinese pedlars were fined for violating it.

Within years, however, the city government confessed to little success in suppressing the pedlars. In 1914 city hall tried unsuccessfully to tax the pedlars and to limit their working hours.

Chang Yun Ho became a pedlar when he bought a route from a friend. His most important investment was his horse: "His backbone was higher than my shoulder, and he took a lot of care. Morning and night I washed the dung and mud off him. Every week I scrubbed him down with soap and gave him good clean-up. It was important to keep him clean all the time so he wouldn't get sick. He cost me more than three hundred dollars. But he was very smart. After one week on my route he knew where to stop of his own accord. I peddled vegetables for fourteen years and I used that horse all the time."

In 1918 the pedlars organized a Vegetable Sellers' Association, just in time to battle a new hundred-dollar licence fee levied against

Cannery worker butchering spring (chinook) salmon.

them. Their lawyer argued that since a pedlar earned only about nine hundred dollars a year and had to pay thirty-eight dollars a month for his horse and wagon, the new fee was excessive. An appeal to the Supreme Court filed by pedlar Chin Sue was refused, but the traders managed to negotiate a reduction to fifty dollars.

Even then, many refused to pay, and over thirty Chinese were arrested and charged in court in September of 1919. But they remained disgruntled because stores paid only ten dollars for a licence. They went on strike, and their lawyer F. M. MacLeod submitted to city council a petition from over five thousand customers calling for a reduction so that the pedlars could resume work. He also went before the city's Finance Committee to argue that the licence would only force customers to pay higher prices. Ordinary people felt they got better prices because the pedlars had lower overhead costs.

But city hall remained adamant. The Chinese had no choice but to pay the fifty-dollar licence fee. After paying, the pedlars demanded additional police protection from thieves who frequently pilfered goods from their wagons.[30]

Working in a Salmon Cannery

The salmon-canning industry was a major employer of Chinese Canadians. In 1900 over forty canneries were lined along the Fraser River near Vancouver. Typically, 75 per cent of a cannery crew were Chinese.

Chinese workers dominated cannery crews for several reasons: the seasonal nature of work (less than five months per year), the lower pay for Chinese workers, and the contract labour system that decreased the risk to cannery owners because the canner paid the Chinese contractor according to the number of cases packed. If the salmon run was low, the canner could

A drum and bugle corps, c. 1920.
These men may have helped raise funds
for Dr. Sun Yat-sen's new government in
China, which faced countless difficulties
during its formative years.

黄寶宗影相館。

money through annual fees, special fund drives, and exit fees levied on returnees. Income was also received from the rental of the association's real estate.

Other ties to China were sparked by dramatic events. In January 1915 Japan made its audacious Twenty-One Demands to seize control of China's military and economic life. The demands, which were accepted by northern dictator Yuan Shih-kai in exchange for Japanese support for his regime, provoked an angry response from Chinese abroad. In Vancouver the Overseas Chinese National Salvation Association called community meetings, raised funds, and pressed for a boycott of Japanese goods. When floods and droughts hit China in 1915, 1920, and 1922, Vancouver's Chinese responded with donations. The 1921 campaign to aid five stricken provinces in north China was well publicized: Chinese restaurants donated a day's lunch income, children donated their New Year's lucky money, and shingle mill crews pledged a day's wages.[22]

Two powerful organizations here gave shape and substance to the politics of China. One was the Chinese Freemasons, who by 1914 had forty branches and twenty thousand members across Canada. The other major political organization was the Kuomintang, founded in China by Dr. Sun Yat-sen, who established a southern revolutionary government in Guangzhou in 1917. The Kuomintang set up branches throughout Canada called the Chinese Nationalist League and established its own newspaper. It quickly became pitted against Dr. Sun's former allies, the Chinese Freemasons, who also had their own newspaper and who expected rewards from China in return for supporting Dr. Sun.

Another area of organization was work-related. In 1916 the Canada Chinese Labour Association was formed in Vancouver. By 1918 it had nearly six hundred members. Open to all Chinese workers, its aims were to improve workers' knowledge and to increase their authority in the

(The well-known) Wo Fat & Company Bakery, label for mooncakes.

---

default on his contractor. The contractor, in turn, could pass his loss onto the workers through room and board deductions.

By 1913 canners were mechanizing their plants to reduce the rising costs of Chinese labour. The Iron Chink, a butchering machine, replaced thirty skilled workers. Automatic can-making machines and a sanitary canning system displaced even more labourers.

Jimmy Hing started out at a cannery unloading fish from the scows. He became a butcher, a timekeeper, and finally floor manager of the Anglo-British Columbia Packing Company. He notes that before the machines came in, the most important workers were the butchers: "An experienced butcher will do about four or five fish a minute. They have to cut off the head, open

Jimmy Hing, 1987.

the belly, and take off the fins. They're really going fast. They have two knives: they use one knife for two or three hours and when it gets dull, they change knives and keep on going until noon time. As soon as they eat, they touch the knives up again.

"The company supplies the knives, but some fussy ones bring their own. The experienced butchers have four or five knives to themselves. They

Canadian-born Earle Chang, a cousin to the
Cumyow family, took flying lessons, 1922.

sharpen them their own way, the way they like, razor sharp. When they slice through the fish you can hear it, whssst, right through! Hear it sing!''

As long as loads of salmon came into the cannery, the contractor fed workers three daily meals of rice, meat, and vegetables. But on slack days, he provided only breakfast at 9 A.M. and supper at 4 P.M. At night, there was gambling in the bunkhouses. Jimmy Hing recalls: ''The men gambled every night: *mah-jong, pai-gow,* fifteen-*wu,* those three games. But it was for very low stakes.''

Alcohol was another problem in the bunkhouses. Cannery contracts up to the 1930s stipulated that contractors would forfeit one hundred dollars to the canner if workers were caught selling liquor. In some cases, the canner could search the contractor's gangs to confiscate liquor.

''The good boys made a few bucks and saved it, and they went back to China every three or four years,'' recounts Jimmy Hing. ''But those who liked to gamble, the lazy ones, the ones who drank—they never went back.''

Working in a Shingle Mill

Chinese-Canadian shingle-mill workers went on their first strike in July of 1917. White workers had persuaded them to go out for shorter working hours. Since the Chinese formed 70 per cent of the workforce, the strikers briefly closed most of the shingle factories in Vancouver and New Westminster.

Working conditions in the shingle mills were dismal and

Men whipsawing timber, Britannia Beach, 1921.

living conditions were primitive. The company supplied bunkhouses, but the workers brought their own blankets. There were no tubs for bathing. For toilets, the men squatted outside. Jung Hong-len started working in a mill in 1915 and recalls that the noise of the huge saws was only one problem:

The mill had so many mosquitoes, you had to wrap up your face to work there. The sky would get dark, with so many mosquitoes! When you wanted to eat, you had to buy powder and light it before eating.

The stronger men were faster, and they earned more money—eleven cents a thousand shingles. You did ten thousand and earned a dollar or so. The cutter had to work fast, so he'd find someone who could pack fast enough for him. If you cut fast, you want a fast packer. If you cut slow, you get a slow packer.

If the mill was looking for help, I'd introduce my kin. You learned by watching, by

helping others. If someone let you learn, you were smiling! But still you were standing in their way! They were suffering, working hard. It was good friends or relatives who let you learn. How long did it take to learn? It depended on whether you were fast or not! Whether your brain remembered or not! You had to know how to calculate.

Once you worked in the shingle mill, you always worked there, because no other work gave you as much money. Did I like it? You just had to be careful! The whites didn't like the work, because

Chinese workers in a shingle mill, Sechelt.

they were afraid to lose their fingers.

The issue that sparked a long strike in 1919 was pay reductions. Machine operators lost two cents per thousand pieces cut, packers lost one cent per thousand pieces, and general labourers lost ten cents per dollar earned. The newly formed Chinese Shingle Workers' Union of Canada organized the strike and set up offices in Chinatown. The employers responded by starting a school to train war veterans to replace the Chinese, but the plan failed. When the strike ended a month later, the workers had recovered their original wages. Confident now, they demanded higher wages in May to compensate for strike losses and won again. The union also advocated higher wages for part-time workers.

The following year the union appointed representatives to every mill. Workers struck at one factory to protest poor treatment from the owner and at another to protest the assault of a fellow worker. When the factories reduced output in May, workers retained their original wages and struck at the one factory that refused to maintain them.

But the economic downturn weakened worker solidarity. In January of 1921 dismissals and wage cuts were underway. When workers struck at one factory to protest lowered wages, strikebreakers came in to take their jobs. At another work site a Chinese worker was reportedly stabbed for refusing to join the strikers, and other nonstrikers asked for police protection.[31]

The First Canadian-born Generation

Canadian-born Chinese grew to adulthood between two worlds. Canada did not accept them as full citizens, while China was an ocean away. As well, they felt disadvantaged for having grown up in Chinatown. Dick Yip, born here in 1907, recalls: "It was hard to get a high school education. A lot of people didn't get it because there was a very tough examination called the junior matriculation. Being brought up in Chinatown had its disadvantages because you didn't communicate with any Canadian people, and therefore you didn't speak English properly. And you didn't have any knowledge of the Bible and those kinds of things. Our parents were the old Chinese types. All the time we went to English school, we went to Chinese school at night."

Those young adults fortunate enough to acquire an education, still faced daunting obstacles. Gordon Won Cumyow aspired to be a lawyer. Through his father, who was a court interpreter, he met solicitors willing to article

Young Canadian-borns and their friends at the Hollow Tree in Stanley Park.

Workers at Sweeney Cooperage, 1911.

Merchants Bank of Canada, Chinatown branch on Carrall Street, 1919. From left: Gordon and Harry Cumyow, Tyson Goon, Earle Chang, and other unidentified bank staff. The Merchants Bank was later absorbed into the Bank of Montreal.

him as a clerk. He worked in their law offices for over two years, but still the Law Society would not accept his application.

He finally resigned when his employer told him, "Cumyow, you're wasting your time, you're not going to get anywhere. You'd better change your profession. If you want to fight them, you've got to have money, you've got to get good lawyers. Because if you succeed, there'll be a hundred behind you, wanting to join up!"

One bright spot in this gloomy picture was that the few Chinese families here tended to be those of merchants and the well-to-do. This lessened the pressure to find work immediately. As Dick Yip put it, "My parents were pretty well off, so I wasn't worrying about starving."

Still, Canadian-born Chinese Canadians were ambitious and restless. In their frustration, some turned towards China. Kew Yip was one of merchant Yip Sang's nineteen sons: "I don't like the whites. I hate them like the devil. I didn't want to learn their stuff. You read the history and see what they did. They pumped all that opium into China, that's what they did! I quit high school, after one year or so. Then I went to China, to Canton where my sister was."

But the political unrest there drove Kew to Hong Kong instead, where he studied Chinese. One day, after the class had submitted essays, his school chum nudged him and said, "The teacher hung yours up as the best!"

Kew fondly recalls, "The

teacher called me up and asked where I was from, so I told him, 'From Canada, Saltwater City.' And he asked, 'Who were your instructors?' When I told him, he laughed and said, 'Your teacher and I were classmates!'"

China gave some Canadian-born Chinese people like Kew a social and cultural context in which they felt comfortable. But it did not work for everyone. Dick Yip comments: "Many went back to China, but they couldn't find work there, either. China wanted people with experience there. They didn't want to hire you. Before, everybody would say, 'Oh, you can always go back to China!' But the Chinese in China looked at the overseas Chinese as a different kind of people. I used to think the people over here were pretty smart. But I found out that the Chinese from China are pretty smart, too."

Canadian-born Women

Whether they tried to be nurses or secretaries, Canadian-born women faced strong opposition. For many years there were no Chinese nurses in British Columbia. Gordon Cumyow recalls:

My sister Aylene wanted to become a nurse. She finished high school and tried again and again to get into nursing school, but they wouldn't take her. My dad tried all the well-known white doctors. No dice. My other sisters wanted to get in, too, but they couldn't. After that, they took up stenography. But it was hard to get into an office also because they said, "We're doing white people's business, why would we hire Chinese?"

Like other young adults, Canadian-born women had dreams and ambitions of their own. Anna Fong Lam, who later graduated as the province's first Chinese-

Canadian nurse, had originally wanted to be a concert pianist:

I used to practise hours every day. I didn't do anything else but practise. I didn't take my exams for the degree, but I had reached that level. I enjoyed it very much, it was my first love. But I realized it wasn't easy. You had to be just tops.

Canadian-born women also went to China and did well. Susanne Yip, merchant Yip

Anna Lam, the first Chinese nurse to graduate in British Columbia, 1930.

Sang's youngest daughter, attended Columbia University in New York. She graduated with a Bachelor of Science degree in 1921 and got a Master's degree in 1922, then went to teach in China. In 1931 she became principal of the Guangdong Provincial First Girls' School.

Mrs. Yat Leong Chang was born in Victoria and married into the Sam Kee Company's Chang family. She tells of her experiences in China:

After my father died, we went back to China. In the village, I went to school for two years. Later I went to

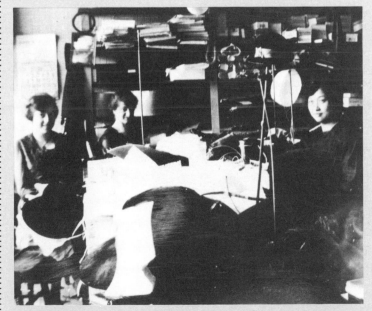

Lillian Ho working in a millinery shop, 1915.

workplace.[23] To educate members it set up Chinese and English language classes, a speechmaking club, and a monthly magazine. When Chinese vegetable pedlars organized themselves in 1918, they met at the association's office. But the premises were soon considered a security risk and were closed by the Canadian government in November. They reopened in May of 1919 shortly before the new Chinese Shingle Workers' Union waged a month-long strike.

On 3 June 1919, a general strike was called by the Vancouver Trades and Labour Council in sympathy with the Winnipeg General Strike. Shipyard, waterfront, streetcar, telephone, and civic workers walked out. Wong Chee Wai of the B.C. Loggers' Union urged Chinese workers to go out, too, to oppose inequality and capitalistic harassment. Strike organizers promised to treat Chinese workers well after the strike and to help them fight discriminatory laws, but there is no evidence to show that the Chinese joined them.[24]

Other changes in Chinatown involved its leadership. For many years, wealthy merchants associated with the Chinese Empire Reform Association had dominated the Chinese Benevolent Association, the chief voice of the community. When the Kuomintang came on the scene in 1912, it elected twelve of its members to the twenty-seat CBA board. Then the constitution was changed to allocate seats according to Old Country home-district associations. This allowed more constituents to be directly represented on the CBA and spelled the end of the Chinese Empire Reform Association.[25]

Even then, the CBA was not the sole representative of the Chinese community. The Chinese consul had offices in Vancouver and acted for the Chinese too. While the CBA and the consul worked together to protest issues such as school segregation, the consul was more likely to have direct dealings with government officials. For example, the consul received and issued news about changes in federal immigration

The Chinese built this arch in honour of the Duke of Connaught's visit to Vancouver in 1912.

Susanne Yip, c. 1921.

Canton looking for a teacher, and then to Macao. I found an excellent teacher. He taught well and I wanted to learn. Why was I so intent on learning? I was so young, what else could I do? I really wanted to be a doctor, I wanted to do something with heart in it. But I never had the opportunity. They wouldn't let me. The women said, "You can't let this girl be a doctor and go around cutting people open!"

I was in Macao for a year, and then I had to get married. I didn't want to get married, I wanted to study. But my mother forced me, she wanted me to get married. Leong's father really liked me. He really wanted me for his daughter-in-law. At the wedding, he wouldn't let the men tease me too much. About Chang Toy's sons, they said, "One's married in Canton, one's married in Saltwater City, so

this one has to be married in the village so that we can invite the folks from all around."

Not all Canadian-born Chinese women came from well-to-do families. Lillian Ho Wong's father died, so she worked to support her mother and family. After working in a millinery shop, she returned to work for Chinese Canadians until she married:

At the back of the Dominion Trust building, there were two

歡迎

WELCOME

Chinese Methodist Mission, kindergarten graduation class, c. 1918. The teachers included Phoebe Chan and Lily McCargar.

restaurants run by men named Mah. Aunty Fong Sai told me to go work there as a waitress for seven dollars a week. The white customers were pretty gentle, they didn't bother you. I always gave them good service, and sometimes they tipped me.

Broken-Mouth Jim came in and made me wait on him after work. He wanted to look me over. I was so mad! I ran off. He wanted me to work for him in Chinatown. I told Mama and she bawled him out. "You think she's like the girls who can't speak English? They're scared, but we're not. I'll go to the police!"

I went to work at the Hong Kong Restaurant, the Peking Restaurant, and the Tianjian Restaurant. After that, I got married. Mama said, "This is a good match, you go." I was about twenty.

The Methodist Young People's Athletic Club, 1924. The churches tried to offer recreational opportunities to the men of Chinatown.

Chinatown Churches

Among the whites, the best friends of the Chinese were church people. By 1923 there were four missions in Chinatown, one Methodist, one Presbyterian, and two Anglican. Church people crusaded for the Chinese in many ways. In 1922 Rev. D. A. Smith of the Chinese Presbyterian Church approached two churches in south Vancouver for room to hold English classes. He wrote of the difficulties encountered: "The former refused to let us have the place as some of the members objected to sitting in the church seats after the Chinese—while the other decided we could not have the Methodist Hall after a meeting so strong that many members left over the business."

Chinese-speaking Hilda Hellaby of the Chinese Anglican Mission worked a very busy schedule. She taught kindergarten every morning, visited at-home women and hospital patients, conducted services twice monthly to sixty Chinese prisoners at Oakalla, distributed tracts, and also taught English at night school and music to Chinese girls.

In 1921 four Missionary Sisters of the Immaculate Conception arrived in Vancouver from Montreal to start a school for Chinese children. These white nuns opened a medical dispensary in 1924 that quickly turned into a small hospital with eighteen beds. Four years later, a hospital building was constructed at 236 Campbell Avenue; this was the predecessor to Mount Saint Joseph Hospital.

While Chinese pastors such as Chan Sing-kai and Fong Dickman had always worked in the Chinatown Mission, discontent still cropped up. In 1911 some Chinese members broke away from the Methodist Mission because they resented the fact that a non-Chinese superintendent controlled the funds that they raised. They formed Christ Church of China, the first independent Chinese Christian Church in Canada. At first, preaching duties were shared by its fifty members because there was no money to hire a pastor. Another rebel church was the Independent Presbyterian Chinese Mission, which later joined Christ Church of China.

Chinese-Canadian Christians were a determined lot. Many parents regarded the Chinese Public School as Confucian, anti-Christian, and reactionary, and therefore established separate schools with Christian Chinese teachers. This was no minor issue, because between 1909 and 1919, the number of children under eighteen years old grew from 230 to 1,000. And Christian converts were often disparaged by the rest of the community.

The Truth About Opium

A new social problem captured public concern in the early 1920s. Abuse of addictive drugs was rising, a generation of youth seemed threatened, and politicians blamed the Chinese. Vancouver Member of Parliament Leon Ladner said in the House of Commons in 1922:

Here we have a disease, one of many directly traceable to the Asiatic. Do away with the Asiatic and you have more than saved the souls and bodies of thousands of young men and women who are yearly being sent to a living hell. . . . Chinamen of great wealth and living in expensive, luxurious quarters give parties at which white women whom they employ act as hostesses. Young girls are invited, and interspersed among these young people are two or three addicts who are trained to inveigle other people into the use of narcotics.

It was true that the early Chinese smoked opium, and several Chinese merchants legally cooked and sold the drug in Victoria, New Westminster, and Vancouver. Few Canadian-born Chinese acquired the habit. In China, several campaigns undertook to eradicate its use there. Then in 1908 the manufacture and sale of opium was banned in Canada, and the drug was subsequently smuggled by Chinese into the country.

From 1900 on, cocaine and heroin abuse spread in the underworld and began to receive press coverage. But newspapers rarely distinguished between heroin and cocaine. Heroin, derived from opium, is a quieting opiate that slows metabolism and soothes pain. Cocaine, derived from coca leaves, is a stimulant that causes nervousness, bizarre behaviour, and paranoia. The unpredictability of cocaine frightened people, and Judge Emily Murphy denounced its use:

DANGER

To the White People of Vancouver

We, the White Taxi-cab Owners and Operators in the City of Vancouver, call upon the white population of the city to support us with their patronage in preference to the Oriental taxi concerns.

We are out to keep the taxi business in Vancouver

Free From the Dope Evil

and to PROTECT THE YOUNGER GENERATION.

We aim especially to give protection and courtesy to white women.
When calling for a taxi the following list will guide you:

Term. City & Motor Co. Sey. 26, 27, 28	Princess Taxi ....Sey. 266
Georgia Taxi Co. ....Sey. 96	Owl Taxi Service ....Sey. 246
Tram Taxi ....Sey. 373	Collins Taxi ....Sey. 27
Seymour Street Taxi ....Sey. 44	Appleby Taxi ....Sey. 179
City Taxi, Auto & Sightseeing	MacLure Auto & Taxi Service
Co., Ltd. ....Sey. 75	............Sey. 26 or Sey. 2606
Tourist Auto Livery Co. ....Sey. 864	Strachan Taxi ....Fair. 2007
Delmonico Taxi ....Sey. 253	Harry Hooper's Taxi ....Sey. 267
Pat's Taxi ....Sey. 152	Cook's Taxi ....Sey. 245
Central Taxi & Auto Service.Sey. 46	Ever-Ready Taxi ....Sey. 1200
Columbia Taxi Co. ....Sey. 757	Stanley Steam Taxi ....Sey. 2077

WHITE TAXI-CAB OWNERS OF VANCOUVER

Anti-dope advertisement from *Danger: The Anti-Asiatic Weekly*, 1921.

A group of performers in opera costume, 1923. Opera was extremely popular amongst the Chinese. The stories of war, love, and tragedy entertained and also reinforced Confucian values. Duty, loyalty and honesty always triumphed, just as they were supposed to in daily life.

regulations, he met with city council over the vegetable pedlars' protest, and he wrote to the mayor regarding inflammatory anti-Chinese articles in the newspaper.

The CBA's concerns certainly overlapped with those of the consul. For example, the association urged city hall to extend business hours for Chinatown stores to allow wifeless workers to shop after a day's work.[26] But the organization's broader interest was for the general welfare of community members and for public relations. It ran a hospital in its building and provided classroom space for the Chinese Public School, which opened in 1917. It raised money for relief of the 1918 Halifax harbour disaster and encouraged Chinese Canadians to donate to the Red Cross and city orphanage fundraising drives. It also appointed an inspector of Chinese patients confined to the city hospital.[27]

Vancouver's Chinese Canadians became more outspoken not only because of white racism but also because of international developments. In China, patriotic mass movements had erupted after World War I when the European powers forced China to cede Shandong province to Japan in the postwar peace talks. These nationalists groped for new cultural definitions of China that would make it strong. For example, the May Fourth Movement, which began in 1919, criticized Confucianism as irrelevant to the needs of twentieth-century nationhood.

Locally, different interest groups emerged. The community had seen its members go off to fight in Europe during World War I alongside white soldiers in defence of Canada. Canadian-borns were reaching adulthood and looking for work in a world that saw them as Chinese, not Canadian; some of them responded by forming a championship soccer team that played as equals against whites on the field. On the other hand, immigrants in Chinatown were keenly focussed on China's culture; in 1914 music enthusiasts formed a club to popularize and improve Cantonese opera songs. At the same time, during these last years of immigration Vancouver became the centre of the Chinese presence in Canada. Although the Canadian-born and immigrants developed different ambitions and different connections to China, they were united by a determination to survive.

"Addicts are immune to pain, they become raving maniacs and are liable to kill or indulge in any form of violence without any sense of moral responsibility."

China was not the major source of drugs, and the police knew this. Church historian Neville Ward fairly summarized the situation:

Contrary to popular opinion, the Chinese are not importers of cocaine, morphine, and heroin, the use of which is becoming increasingly prevalent among the white population. These come from central Europe and the traffic in large quantities is in the hands of white men. Raw opium, such as is smoked by the Chinese themselves, does come from China, but its use is practically restricted to the Chinese.

The Chinese, however, have been used considerably as distributors of narcotics by those engaged in the business on a large scale. The spread of the habit amongst the white people has been attributed to the Chinese by their antagonists, and has been advanced as an additional reason for their exclusion. As a matter of fact, the habit has arisen, quite apart from the influence of the Chinese, from a demand characteristic of the age for a swift artificial stimulant to the senses and emotions.

In Vancouver, the police admitted that although the drug habit had been growing, it was certainly not growing any more rapidly than in other cities proportionate to population. But local notoriety grew because news reports highlighted the arrests of several large-scale drug dealers who were Chinese.[32]

The Reverend Andrew Roddan (left) of First United Church visits Chinese squatters at a makeshift cookhouse in the False Creek Flats "jungle," where homeless men lived, 1931.

Hard Times: Racism, Depression and War

For years to come, from the 1923 Chinese exclusion act until the end of World War II, Chinese Canadians faced hard times on many fronts. Despite their gradually declining numbers, they were viewed as an economic and racial threat and Chinatown was seen as immoral and crime-infested. At mid-century, however, things began to change, albeit slowly.

One galling feature of the 1923 exclusion law called for every person of Chinese descent to register with the Immigration Department. It did not matter where one was born or how long one had been here. Many older Chinese Canadians possessed no documents proving legal entry and Canadian-borns often had no birth certificates. Won Alexander Cumyow, for example, was born at Fort Douglas in 1860, well before Canadian confederation.[1]

White Canada had succeeded in stopping Chinese immigration. The handful of arrivals between 1923 and 1947 were teachers, church personnel, and consular staff. But even this success failed to placate white critics. During the sensational 1924 Janet Smith murder scandal, in which a Chinese houseboy was wrongfully accused of killing a white maid, Scottish organizations demanded a law forbidding white women and Chinese Canadians from working in the same house. In 1925 the Hotel Vancouver replaced its Chinese-Canadian workers with whites. With the introduction of minimum wage laws for

sawmills in 1926, many Chinese Canadians were dismissed. In 1927 the Ku Klux Klan chapter in Vancouver called for governments to end Asian immigration, to send all Asians back to Asia, and to expropriate their property here. In 1928 restaurant workers also fell under minimum wage legislation, which further discouraged the hiring of Chinese workers since they would have to be paid the same as whites.[2]

Community Trends

Most of Vancouver's Chinese Canadians remained in Chinatown and Strathcona in the decades after the immigration was halted. No new construction occurred there before the end of World War II, nor did Strathcona become all-Chinese. Instead, it remained a multiethnic district of Japanese, Jews, Blacks, and eastern Europeans. Chinatown was a ghetto, a community with its own separate life. The theatres, restaurants, and gaming halls were crowded, while children played in the streets. In 1928 the Chinese Benevolent Association raised three thousand dollars to equip a children's playground on the railway lands at Pender and Carrall.[3] This effort pointed to one notable change after 1921: the children and teenagers of Chinatown tended to be Canadian-born rather than immigrant.

The community comprised merchants' families and "bachelor" labourers. The families were likely to buy houses and modern appliances;

Opening of the Chinese Playground, 1928, behind the southeast corner of Pender and Carrall streets. Standing by the stage is Won Alexander Cumyow, and on stage is Mayor L. D. Taylor.

The Janet Smith Mystery

On 26 July 1924, Wong Foon Sing, a houseboy in a Shaughnessy home, found young nursemaid Janet Smith dead in the basement from a gunshot wound to her head. An inquest ruled it an accidental death, but the United Council of Scottish Societies pressed for a second inquest. In the interim Wong was bundled off by a group of private detectives and policemen who interrogated and beat him. Then the second inquest concluded that Smith could not have killed herself accidentally. Now it became a sensationalized murder case with no suspects, and the Chinese houseboy immediately became the scapegoat.

The rumour mill was churning: Smith was killed at a wild high-society party; Smith was raped and then killed; or Smith was killed by leaders of

Houseboy Wong Foon Sing, accused of the murder of Janet Smith. From *Vancouver Sun*, 1 May 1925

**Victoria Produce store at
1743 Commercial Drive, 1932.**

their children were educated at English and Chinese schools. Wealthier families often sent their children to China for their education; less able families went on relief during the Depression. Labourers' families were in China, so the men lived thriftily, saving every penny to send home. They took regular trips back: from 1926 to 1935, Chinese Canadians made thirty-two thousand visits to China. The newspapers warned travellers of unscrupulous Chinese aboard ship who would fleece them of their savings. In 1930 one hapless man lost eight thousand dollars while gambling en route.[4]

Chinese Canadians soon dominated the greengrocery business in the city. The 52 Chinese greengrocers of 1923 increased to 125 by 1935, out of a total of 158 stores. However, the number of Chinese laundries and Chinese-run Canadian-food cafés located outside Chinatown decreased during the same period, although the number of Chinese-food restaurants in Chinatown grew.[5] The strongest growth occurred

the narcotics trade. Then, on the night of 20 March 1925, Wong suddenly vanished.

Six weeks later Wong was found one morning wandering the streets of Point Grey. He had been severely beaten. Amazingly, he was now charged with murder.

Wong said that three men had seized him one night when his employer was out. They blindfolded him, tied his arms and took him for a long car ride

to a house. The next morning, two men dressed in white robes with hoods over their heads questioned him. When he couldn't tell them who had killed Smith, they began to beat him.

Over the weeks, the physical attacks intensified. Wong lost his hearing in one ear and his vision blurred. At one point he was dragged to an attic, where a heavy rope was strung over a beam. The rope was tightened

around his neck, and Wong was forced to stand atop a stool while the men pulled at the rope and acted as if they were going to kick the stool out.

In June, twelve people were indicted for kidnapping Wong: operatives of the Canadian Detective Bureau, several members of the Point Grey Police Force, and three members of the Scottish societies. Most of the twelve

were later acquitted.

When Wong came before the grand jury that fall, the jurors found insufficient evidence against him and released him. In March of 1926, Wong returned to China. To this day, no one knows who killed Janet Smith.

For a detailed account of this event, see Edward Starkins's book, *Who Killed Janet Smith?* (Toronto: Macmillan of Canada, 1984).

Chinese School

Chinese school was very important to parents in the twenties and thirties. As Anne Loo's mother put it, "You're Chinese, how can you not know the Chinese language?" But the Canadian-borns were not that keen. Anne Loo recalls how they responded:

My younger brothers and sisters weren't impressed with what she said. But still, we all went. I couldn't say that I

Members of the Chinese Student concert in aid of the U.B.C. Stadium Fund, Feb. 20, 1931.

Chinese-Canadian students at the University of British Columbia, 1931. University degrees from this period, however, did not open doors into mainstream jobs and careers.

learned much. It intruded on my time. In high school, my PE teacher said I'd make a very good goalie in the grass hockey team. But I said to her, "Gee, I wish I could stay after school and practise, but I can't because I've got to go to Chinese School."

By 1937 Vancouver's ten Chinese schools had an enrolment of about seven hundred. In addition to the Chinese Public School on

Tommy Ming Lum at Canada Produce,
Granville Street, c. 1940.

HARD TIMES

· · · · ·
79

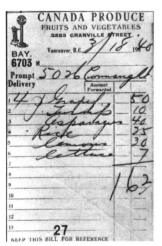

Canada Produce (grocery store) receipts, 1940.

among Chinese-Canadian fruit and vegetable wholesalers, increasing from one in 1922 to twenty-one in 1936. And where there was growth, there was trouble.

Against the Grocers

Chinese-Canadian greengrocers had long been a target of white racism. Because they offered lower prices, convenient hours, and fresh merchandise attractively displayed, they were seen as a threat to white stores, and there were calls to segregate Chinese stores and to enforce sanitation and closing-hour laws against them.[6]

In 1928, 143 Vancouver businessmen, including executives from the three largest department stores, petitioned Victoria to let municipal governments limit the number of shops owned by nonwhites. A Trades Licences Board Act was passed to permit such boards to refuse licences it deemed against the public interest. W. H. Malkin, a leading wholesale grocer, became mayor of Vancouver, and one

unsuccessful plank of his campaign was that "Oriental shops should be confined to fixed Oriental areas."[7] In 1929 some Chinese-Canadian storekeepers decided to stop doing business on Sundays to avoid further anti-Chinese agitation.[8] Throughout the Depression years, their businesses suffered from recurring robberies.

Against the Farmers

In 1927 provincial laws were passed to regulate the marketing of tree fruits and vegetables, which meant that the volume of farm produce allowed onto the market, as well as its selling price, were now set by a board. Chinese-Canadian farmers, wholesalers, pedlars, and storekeepers saw this as a move to limit and reduce their business activity and quickly protested. They claimed that the board raised prices to consumers and reduced the producers' return.[9] The Chinese consul met with provincial officials, and Chinese farmers announced that they would challenge the law in London.

Pender Street, classes were sponsored by family associations, by the Freemasons, and by churches. They provided only elementary school language classes until after World War II, when the Mon Keang School started secondary classes.

The teachers were hired from China; they entered under exemptions from the exclusion law. Wong Kown Fow was a teacher and

principal at Mon Keang School from 1936 to 1969. He was particularly interested in teaching speaking skills:

Every week, we had public-speaking sessions. No matter whether they told stories or recited essays, they had to stand up and speak. Every student took a turn, to practise pronunciation. Then we trained them to do plays. They had to speak properly in order to move the audience. Some

plays even had opera songs in them. There was no music, just solo singing.

You had to have enthusiasm to do the plays. If the students had heart and could show it, then everyone applauded. It took a lot from the students! But the students were older, they were high school students about to graduate, so it was easier to work with them. In those days, many were still intending to go back to China,

so the students were very attentive.

Most of Vancouver's Chinese spoke dialects from the rural Say-yup region, whereas the city dialect of Cantonese tended to be recognized as an official tongue. Wong Kown Fow:

Officially we used Cantonese, but the teachers like me used half Cantonese and half Toisanese. So it became a Wah Kew Wah, an

Workers sorting vegetables in a produce warehouse, c. 1925.

They and the wholesalers flouted the regulations and several court cases ensued.[10]

In 1934 the B.C. Coast Vegetable Marketing Board was set up, and physical confrontations erupted when the police barricaded the bridges into town to stop Chinese farmers from delivering their produce to wholesalers. In August of 1935 fourteen Chinese potato trucks crashed the barriers at the Marpole Bridge. The farmers were brought to court but released because the Crown could not prove that the produce was being transported for local sale.[11]

Farmer Sing Lee charged a provincial police constable and a board inspector with assault. Lee testified that they ordered him to unload twenty-five sacks of potatoes from his truck at the Queensborough Bridge, but he refused because the sacks were tagged for export. The two officials followed him to his farm, where they struck his head and arms with iron bars.[12]

In June 1936 the board began seizing shipments of potatoes stored in Vancouver warehouses. Ladner farmers Chung Chuck and Mah Lai went to the Supreme Court for an injunction to restrain the board. They claimed they were merely storing their potatoes in Vancouver for export.[13] When the board continued to stop trucks entering Vancouver, the farmers asked that board officials be jailed for contempt of court. At the same time, 150 Chinese pedlars petitioned city council to protect them against board inspectors, who were allegedly dumping their potatoes onto the street for "inspection" purposes.[14]

In January 1937 the Privy Council ruled that federal laws on marketing boards were invalid, and this prompted Chinese-Canadian farmers and wholesalers to sue the board for levies it had unlawfully collected.[15] But white farmers denounced the Chinese as unfair competitors who defied regulations over prices, hours of work, and minimum wages. In March these white farmers mounted twenty-four-hour pickets on all four bridges leading

overseas Chinese dialect. Cantonese speakers were few at that time, even among the parents. So you could teach Cantonese, but if the parents spoke Toisanese, there was conflict.

The Greengrocer's Work
Tommy Ming Lum came to Canada in 1923 at the age of thirteen and in 1927 opened his second grocery store, the Canada Produce, at Thirteenth Avenue and Granville Street. He recalls:

In those days it wasn't self-service. People walked into the store and told you what they wanted, you wrote it down, and then you ran around and filled their order. They phoned

Tommy Ming Lum, 1987.

in orders and we delivered. The way we did business, gathering orders and delivering and giving credit, it was a real bargain for the customers.

There were two other stores on the block, so there was competition. In those days, we didn't have walk-in coolers, so you had to lower your price before the goods went bad. But if I sold cheap, they sold cheap, too. Everyone lost money that way.

To make our money we had to work 365 days of the year. It was busy and there were long hours. Even if I didn't go to sleep, there was work to do. We lived behind the store. In the winter we had no heat. It was so cold that I got chilblains on my hands and feet.

Wartime shortages made it hard to get stock. So if Safeway had mayonnaise, I would go and buy it one jar at a time and bring it to my back room. Then I would have stock to sell, but only to my good customers. There was price control: inspectors came by to check the prices. You could only mark up a certain percentage. If you exceeded it, you got punished.

I was pretty stupid, arranging the fruit over and over! I used oranges to spell out the name of our store. Then I had to replace the fruit when it went bad. So much time and energy spent and not much return!

Wing and Anne Loo ran the South Van Produce store at 1057 Denman Street for forty-three years, selling only fresh fruits, vegetables and flowers. They were known to carry the best quality in town.

We were busy all the time, from morning until night. I don't wish it onto anybody. No choice! You either work or die!

I was in the restaurant and grocery business but the easiest to get along in is the produce business, because most of the customers are ladies. In the restaurant business you get drunks and people who come in and eat and won't pay, and there are fights.

When my husband went to the wholesalers to buy, he didn't care about the price very much. He wanted the best quality. He looked everything

Chinese News Weekly, Canada's first English-language Chinese-Canadian newspaper, 1936.

into Vancouver to stop the Chinese "bootleggers." Some twenty men, for example, guarded the Marpole Bridge. After Chung Chuck tried unsuccessfully to barrel through, he charged an inspector and six Richmond farmers with assault. They in turn charged Chung with assault.[16]

While the marketing boards insisted that they did not intend to discriminate against the Chinese, it was hard to divorce the economic issue from the racial one. Newspapers, as in this *Province* editorial of 2 March 1937, warned against a Chinese "takeover" of the industry:

A decade ago Orientals were content to turn over their vegetable, farm and small fruit products to the ordinary channels of trade in Vancouver and take whatever was the ruling price for that commodity. Today the situation has vitally changed. Production and marketing of all these household necessities is directed by smart young Orientals, born in Vancouver and claiming all the rights and privileges of Canadian citizenship.

Twenty years ago lowly John Chinaman leased a parcel of land from its white owner and, mostly by hand, produced what he could peddle through the streets of the town. Today that picture is quite outmoded. Big Chinese corporations own large farms, equipped with up-to-date machinery, but still manned by the cheapest Oriental labor, working from dawn to dark; and their produce is sent to market in trucks owned by Orientals, driven by Oriental chauffeurs, delivered to Oriental warehouses, sold finally through Oriental retail stores—where the salesgirl is very apt to be a brilliant young Chinese graduate of the University of B.C. It is a changed situation indeed!

Chinese have crossed into the imported vegetable market as well. Wholesale Row of Water Street, supposed to contain some of the cleverest men engaged in the business, has had to make peace with the Chinese invaders. How long will it be before the

over and only bought the best. And he charged accordingly. And if people couldn't afford it, well, they'd have to shop elsewhere. But there were other people who wanted top quality—good, fresh merchandise—and they knew they could get it from our place. And they were willing to pay good prices.

People all over Vancouver knew our store. I'm not bragging, it's the truth. They knew that we had what they wanted. "If you can't get it anywhere, go to South Van, you'll get it." And that was true. They'd find stuff that was out of season, that was hard to get, that other shops didn't carry.

There's no trick about it, there's no secret. Just give the customer good service, the right price, and good merchandise, that's all.

Anne and Wing Loo, 1987.

latter are in command of the whole situation?

Against the Gamblers

One night in 1924 David Lew, a Canadian-educated interpreter, was shot to death on Pender Street. It was rumoured that he been killed for his gambling and stool-pigeoning activities. In subsequent weeks the police carried out another clean-up to rid Chinatown of its gambling, opium, and illegal liquor. Coincidentally, the chairman of the city's finance committee proposed moving Chinatown to another location because the site was of industrial importance for its water access.[17] But Chinatown was also associated with the seamier side of life, and its proximity to Skid Row exacerbated things. In 1928, amidst charges of bribery against the police, a special enquiry was appointed. Several Chinese gaming-hall operators testified that they paid protection money to the police, but the commissioner did not believe them.[18]

Gambling had been popular in China and flourished among the "bachelors" of Chinatown, who had no familial or other diversions. It was also encouraged by the fact that Chinese-Canadian workers could find only low-paying jobs on the margins of the economy; lured by the easy money supposedly available from games of chance, they gambled for a win that might let them return to China or start a small business. Certainly, games of chance were just as prevalent elsewhere in the city, but newspaper reports focussed on Chinatown's exotic forms of gambling.

As joblessness began to mount in Chinatown in late 1929, the gambling halls revealed their other functions. To protest police raids, one hall's lawyer informed the police commission that unemployed Chinese Canadians slept and ate there; if the police forced the hall to close, then a hundred elderly Chinese would go on relief. Chinatown's betting, the lawyer pointed out, was no different from that underway in exclusive private white clubs. Despite this, police raids were particularly severe in 1930 and 1931, resulting in the near-starvation of Chinatown's professional gamblers.[19]

Police raids on Chinatown varied in frequency over the years. On one hand, the arrests netted revenue for the city: in one month in 1933, sixteen gaming halls were raided and a total of $1,095 was collected in fines. On the other hand, the police chief feared too many raids would send too many bodies to the city jail and thereby drain city funds.[20] The police use of stool pigeons, sent into gambling halls to check for games of chance and note the proprietor's rake-off, was widely resented by the Chinese, and informers were sometimes beaten.

Against the Cafés

The perception of Chinatown as unsavoury also affected its cafés. The Women and Girls Protection Act of 1924 allowed the police chief to force employers to discharge white females from work that damaged their moral fibre, and in the fall of 1935 three

Growing Up in the Twenties and Thirties

Childhood in old Chinatown was a unique experience. William Chu recalls watching the police raid the gambling halls: "Across the street, there used to be an old house loaded with gamblers. Every other day the paddy wagons came. My brother and sister would sit and count, 'Oh, 180 people!' They loaded them up about twelve to a wagon, took them

Patrice and Dr. William Chu, 1987.

to the police station, and the wagons kept coming back. But before they finished taking the last load, the first one was back and rolling the dice again!"

Chinatown had become a tourist attraction, which proved profitable to children, according to William. "Summertime, the American tourists came. Boy, were they generous! They went to the bank and got a roll of dimes,

An airplane built in Chinatown! In 1935 seventeen-year-old Robert Shun Wong read a magazine article that showed how to build a single-seat Pietenpol airplane with a thirty-foot wingspan. Wong, an experienced model airplane builder, started to build the airplane right in his family's upstairs apartment at 124 Market Alley in Chinatown. The frame was of wood; a used engine was found at an auto wrecker. The pieces were assembled at an adjacent garage and then at the airport. In July 1937 the "Sky Scout" rolled out onto the tarmac. It flew beautifully! Wong flew it regularly until March of 1938 when he left for air college in eastern Canada.

and gave it out to the Chinese kids. Boy, they must have given out ten dollars!''

Most Chinese-Canadian families were not well-to-do so recreation became a very creative affair. Alfred Wong: "On Keefer Street there was only one bicycle, a used one. It was Albert Chin's, but it was the street's bicycle because everybody used it. When we snuck into a theatre, whoever had the money to pay went in and opened the back door so we could get in. Or we'd drill holes through the door and put in a wire and lift the handle off. Sometimes we snuck in through the coal bin, down the coal chute and then underneath the stage and up. So we did have our fun!''

Anne Loo recalls walking a lot: "We'd hike all the way from Cambie and Sixth to Capilano to watch the baseball games. We'd hike across the bridge and go to the movies for five cents on Saturdays at the Dominion. We thought nothing about walking. We never had telephones either. It was amazing how we managed, eh?''

Schooling provided some problems unique to the Chinese. Patrice Chu: "Many girls, like my cousin and those who lived down in Chinatown, didn't go to high school. They went for one year and quit. It cost money, and going suddenly into a high school away from Chinatown was something like coming out of an Indian reserve; it was very difficult to adjust.''

Most parents were exceedingly keen on education. William Chu: "My father felt there was no way out, except through education. He said he was glad if he could have a livelihood enough to bring up ten children, as long as any

Men pushing a shack on wheels. In
November 1935 firemen wrecked and
torched a Chinese "jungle town" under the
Georgia Viaduct near Columbia Street. Eight

shanties and a makeshift tunnel fifty feet
along the Great Northern Railway trestle
housed the homeless.

86

Chinatown café-owners were ordered to fire their white waitresses.[21] The police alleged that young white women prostituted themselves to the Chinese.

Chinatown contained both restaurants serving Chinese food and cafés serving Western food. The restaurants originally employed Chinese waitresses to help cultivate customers. But by the 1930s many of the waitresses who had arrived before 1923 had been married off, and café-owners turned to white girls. Local Chinese families refused to let their daughters work as waitresses:

Chinese waitresses were seen as spoiled, tarnished goods because they catered to the whims of men. Whether they were totally prostitutes or just working as a waitress made no difference at that time. They had to be able to carry on a good conversation and of course these ladies were all painted up. But there were many classes of them. Some were extra friendly, some were very reserved: they would only speak when spoken to. If they were lucky

enough to be married, then they would be a little more straight. Then there were the ones brought over just to work and make money.[22]

When café owners hired white women, the racist nature of the protection act became evident: only white women were to be protected.

In January of 1936 the charges laid under the protection act were dismissed because the police chief had not dealt with each woman individually. The act was found to be ineffective because women were fired before their cases came to trial. So the police turned to the city Licence Department for help and informed eight Chinatown cafés, where some thirty women worked, that applications for 1937 licences would not be granted unless they agreed not to hire any white waitresses.[23]

This infuriated the waitresses, who told the mayor that they could find no work elsewhere. A compromise was then worked out: the cafés would keep them until they left, but no white replacements were to be hired.[24]

Licences were issued, but when three cafes were discovered to have broken the compromise rules, their licences were cancelled.

The café owners fought back. Their lawyer asked for a court injunction against the city,[25] which was refused. At this point the café owners decided to halt the battle in order to promote goodwill, and on 1 October 1937, the cafés dismissed the thirty white women who worked for them. The women, many of whom were supporting families, trekked to city hall along with the Vancouver Mothers' Council to protest again.[26] But the ban continued into 1939, despite further petitions from the women.

Depression Times

When the Great Depression hit, British Columbia was rocked: it suffered higher unemployment than any other province in every job category. With the large number of men in the Chinese-Canadian population, Chinatown faced severe difficulties. In

one of us could do better than he did. That was his philosophy because he saw so much suffering of his own brothers and sisters in China. He said, 'Don't worry about not getting a job here, you can always go back to China!'"

Bill and Jack Wong recall that their childhood summers in the 1930s gave them their first peek at the world outside Chinatown: "We were very fortunate to go to summer

camp. The church subsidized us because we couldn't afford to go. We went to camp for two weeks and mixed with white boys from better homes, from the West End. We were able to associate with them, be friends with them, and that really opened our eyes."

Bill and Jack Wong, 1987.

Mount St. Joseph's Oriental Hospital

Sister Theresa Fung arrived in Vancouver from Canton in April 1936. She was Vancouver's first Chinese nun, and worked with the non-Chinese-speaking Missionary Sisters of the Immaculate Conception who had come from Montreal in 1921. Her base of operations was Mount St. Joseph's Oriental Hospital, established in 1924 to serve the Chinese community. The hospital cared for some sixty tuberculosis patients and twenty elderly homeless men.

People were very afraid of TB then. It was very contagious, there was no cure. So people were afraid to visit; the government didn't allow many visitors. We wore face masks and changed our clothes whenever we served them.

We sisters did everything. We washed the floors, fed the

Sister Theresa Fung, 1987.

patients, did the cooking. A lot of times we went to the Chinese farms and asked for vegetables. We picked our own, especially the badly grown vegetables that the farmers didn't want. We brought them back and did our own canning.

To raise funds I went to all the Chinese stores to ask for donations every year. I even went into the gambling halls, and the men there donated.

Men at a public board reading news and notices, c. 1932. The case on the far left advertised Quene Yip's insurance services. His wife Victoria recalled, "Can you imagine selling insurance during the Depression? Well, what can you do? To draw in business, we used to listen to the radio for war news, and then we translated it into Chinese, wrote it up, and put it up for the people to read. All the people in Chinatown went and read it because it was faster than waiting for the newspaper to come out. We did that every day."

Twenty-five cents in those days was a lot of money.

I was very well treated by the people of Chinatown. Often when I was buying things, maybe a crab for ten cents, they would say, "Here, take it!"

The Chinese Times newspaper was very good to us. For many years they gave us free newspapers and they carried our calls for donations. People from small towns would cut out the newspaper announcement and tape it onto an envelope and send in cash.

Before I came, the sisters did all the cooking with water. They boiled up chicken and rice and vermicelli, and that was considered a Chinese meal. But the men wanted salt fish steamed with pork. They liked the taste of dou-see and meen-see [bean sauces]. They liked roast pork and salt-shrimp sauce and tofu, so one day, I heated the big pot (there were no woks in those days), and fried up the garlic and the salt shrimp. And then the sisters came running, crying, "What are you doing? It stinks!"

The stove used wood and coal. It was hard to cook rice. When the rice boiled over, it doused the coals. And when you reheated the coal, you would sear the bottom of the pot and have burned rice!

In those days, fifteen or twenty or thirty men would pool their money and buy a house to live in together. The thing they feared the most was that someone should die in that house. It was the same with people who owned rooming houses. They were afraid that if someone died in their building, then no one would want to live there. So they would call me in when

GHETTOS FOR CHINESE?

Sir: While your cities are destroyed and your sons and kin die so that democratic freedom may prevail, your "better citizens" of Southlands are only concerned whether they can tolerate a Chinese Canadian to live in their midst. FEB 8 1941

Abetted by able leadership of a man that made Oriental baiting his political career we find this group of democratic Canadian people doing all within their power to prevent the catastrophe of having a Chinese couple as their neighbors.

A while back Ald. Wilson was ranting about the low standard of living of the Orientals. Strange that when any of the second generation Orientals makes a move to fulfill Mr. Wilson's ideals for "better Orientals," his first obstacle is an anemic issue fostered by the very man that extolls the "lamentable squalor" we are supposed to live in.

To you "better citizens" of Southlands, Vancouver, the many petty points I could bring to your attention I will leave alone.

But remember, your motherland England went to the extreme privations of total war to defend the ideals you are so ready to trample upon.

When Mr. Churchill tells you that the Nazi principles of intolerance must be destroyed, you cheer. When Mr. Roosevelt made his inaugural speech that freedom shall prevail for all peoples, you are also in accordance.

A final comment on his worship's statement that, "If anything can be done to segregate them" (Orientals "in the same district, we are all for it."

When people openly commend the policies of Herr Hitler and Herr Streicher, we Chinese are ready for your Ghettos and concentration camps.

A SECOND GENERATION
CHINESE.

1931, 80 per cent of the residents were jobless. Until August of that year the Chinese-Canadian community provided its own relief. Stores donated food, and funds were raised for the unemployed. Even then, Chinese Canadians were arrested for begging on the streets.[27]

By November of 1931, 75 Chinese Canadians were taking city relief and another 260 were destitute. At this point the Chinese Benevolent Association asked the city for help.[28] The city Relief Office gave jobless Chinese men bed and meal tickets, which allowed them to eat in cafés and live in hotels approved by the department. But this treatment was soon to change. To qualify for tickets, all recipients had to agree to join provincial work camps. These road-building camps were set up outside Vancouver and paid workers a dollar a day. Chinese-Canadian relief applicants were excused from these camps because there were no separate accommodations for the Chinese; it was assumed that they and the whites could not share living quarters.[29]

The fact that the Chinese were excused from work-camp duty caused whites to complain. E. W. Griffiths, the city's relief officer, thought—and this was a recurring attitude among relief administrators—that the usual scale of relief should not apply to Chinese Canadians because they could live on half the amount needed by whites. "We can never expect Orientals to become self-supporting or even attempt to look for a job so long as they are getting more on relief than they ever earned in good times," he said.[30]

When the provincial government took charge of the single unemployed, it arranged for the Anglican Chinese Mission to provide shelter and meals for Chinese Canadians. The mission set up a soup kitchen in Chinatown at 143 East Pender Street to serve two daily meals and distribute clothes and shoes. The provincial government allocated sixteen cents a day per man for food and sixty cents a week for shelter. In comparison, meal tickets for whites were worth fifteen to twenty-five cents *each*.[31]

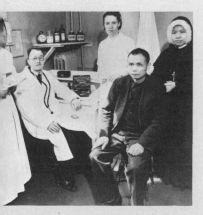

Sister Theresa Fung and Dr. Kew Ghim Yip with a patient at the Chinese Hospital Clinic, 1937.

they had someone really sick. I would go and see, and I could tell if someone was about to die. If that were the case, then I would call a taxi and bring him home and let him die at our hospital.

A lot of the Chinese were afraid that when they died, no one would bury them. They hid money in their clothes, or rolled it up, sewed it up, and tied it around their waist. So when someone came in, I

made sure to check all his clothes before destroying them. We threw the clothes in a big tub of water to kill fleas and things. If there was money, we placed it in our safe. When he died, I would contact his family or county association and say, "Don't worry, there's money for his burial."

This discriminatory treatment was resisted by Chinese and white unemployed workers' groups. In November of 1933 two whites led fifty Chinese Canadians to city hall to demand welfare assistance.[32] In January of 1935 the Provincial Workers Council, together with the Chinese Workers' Protective Association, demanded a raise in food and room allowances. They denounced the soup kitchen food as "insufficient and low grade." A petition containing 520 signatures asked that the soup kitchen be abolished and that the unemployed Chinese Canadians receive relief equal to that of jobless whites.[33] At that time over eleven hundred Chinese were enrolled at the kitchen. When the Young Communists, the Youth CCF, and the Young Socialists joined a protest there in March 1935, policemen guarded the premises against violence; several of the Chinese cooks had reportedly quit because they had been threatened.[34]

Provincial relief was granted only to those were were considered employable.

Those who were not, such as nine elderly and infirm Chinese-Canadian men, were sent to the Anglican Chinese Mission Home. The city relief office paid the nine-dollar monthly fee but refused to inform the recipients that they were doing so because "the city might be forced to bear a much heavier load in this connection if it became generally acknowledged."[35]

The governments preferred to send destitute Chinese Canadians back to China because it was cheaper to pay for transportation than to maintain people on relief over an extended period of time. Passage cost fifty-five dollars in 1935; the city and province each paid half. Those who were repatriated included the destitute, the infirm, the mentally ill, and some widows. To qualify for the repatriation subsidy, the Chinese had to declare that they would never return to Canada. By year's end, some four hundred Chinese Canadians had returned to China under government subsidy.[36]

In 1938 the province transferred the

The Chinese Workers Protective Association and the Unemployed Chinese Association rallied on May Day, 1935, at Larwill Park, to protest the unsatisfactory soup kitchen services offered to needy Chinese.

Chinese Students' Soccer Club with the Mainland Cup, 1934.

Chinese Soccer Champions

During the dark days of racism, one team effort brightened Chinatown's spirit. The Chinese Students' Soccer Club won the Iroquois Cup (1926), the Spalding Cup (1937), the B.C. Mainland Cup (1934), the Wednesday League Cup (1931), and the L. D. Taylor Trophy for sportsmanship. The players were heroes to all Chinatown. They proved that Chinese Canadians could excel at sports and that, unlike the racist situations of daily life, in this arena the Chinese could fight and win.

The team drew its strength from Chinatown's few families such as the Yips, Louies, Cumyows, and Soones, in body count and in morale. "Earle Chang's parents always went to the games," recalled goalie Spoon Wong. "One player pushed Earle and started a fight. Earle's mother

came down with her umbrella and knocked it over his head and knocked him down!''

When the team captured the B.C. Mainland Cup, Chinatown erupted in a wild celebration. A parade with a hired band began at Con Jones Park, car horns blaring. The players held the three-foot-high cup aloft in an open car. Firecrackers exploded in Chinatown, where a crowd of thousands waited. In the midst

of all this, a fire alarm went off and brought two fire trucks out. The next day was declared a holiday in Chinatown, with free tea and *dim-sum* for everyone.

The Chinese players were slight in build, averaging 130 pounds. How did they win? Spoon Wong: ''We were faster. They were big but slow. We ran rings around them. We played a kick-and-run game. As soon as we got the ball, we

kicked it away and chased it. Sometimes we spoke Chinese in the game, shouting things like 'Watch him!' or 'Don't let him through!' The other team didn't know what we were saying, so they sent a letter to the club, asking the president to stop us from speaking Chinese. We went to the meeting and said, 'You speak in English and we don't understand English.' So they let us speak Chinese.''[48]

You Wanna Woman?

For many years Chinatown remained a ''bachelor'' society because the immigration laws blocked men from sending for their wives and families. As any other men with natural sexual appetites would do in such a situation, the ''bachelors'' turned to prostitutes. Canadian-born Lun Yee worked in several Chinatown restaurants and provided free translation services to his

In 1936 Chinatown welcomed the city to its "Carnival Village" to celebrate Vancouver's fiftieth birthday. Left: an eighty-five-foot-high bamboo archway, constructed without a single nail, was brought in from Hong Kong. Right: Chinatown elected its own Jubilee Queen, Grace Kwan, and she met with child movie star Shirley Temple at the site.

"Drums and Dance to Save the Country" read the four big characters on the lower horizontal banner. This stage production was one of many mounted by groups in Chinatown to raise funds for China during the war against Japan, 1932.

Case for B.C. Chinese

Sir: I am one of the hundreds of Canadian-born Chinese, of military age, and glad of the privilege of fighting and dying for Canada.

Here are a few facts I would like to place before the Canadian public to get their opinion on whether it does or does not constitute British fair play.

First—Although my parents are naturalized British subjects for 35 years and myself born in Vancouver, I am not allowed to vote. The government's reason, I am an alien.

Second—Although I possess registered firearms for hunting, I must surrender them by September 30, 1940. The government's reason, I am an alien.

Third—Canada adopts conscription, therefore I am drafted into the Canadian army. The government's reason, I am a British subject.

(Chinese-Canadians were not accepted when they volunteered for active service).

Although the above are all true facts we Chinese-Canadians are willing to accept them, but we feel that we must be given an assurance that a franchise be granted us after serving with Canada's fighting forces.

A copy of this letter is being forwarded to the B. C. and Dominion Government.

C. E. LOUIE.

"Case for B.C. Chinese," newspaper letter to editor, 1940.

job of looking after the needy Chinese Canadians back to the city. By this time, there were 406 Chinese on relief, and the city decided to continue using the services of the Anglican Church Mission.[37] Forty per cent of the Chinese remained unemployed, and only 35 per cent had regular jobs. Many did odd jobs like gardening and wood-chopping, but still relied on others for assistance.[38]

A Long War

While the Depression brought hard times to Vancouver's Chinese Canadians, the news from China was not good, either. In addition to ongoing problems in south China with bandits and natural disasters, Japan invaded Manchuria in September of 1931. In Vancouver, three thousand Chinese attended a mass meeting and launched a boycott of all Japanese goods. In the following months the Chinese here raised sixteen thousand dollars in war aid.[39] Still, full-scale war did not break out because China's Chiang Kai-shek chose not to resist the Japanese but

instead to exterminate the Chinese Communists. The Japanese penetrated deeper into north China until 1937, when Chiang finally formed a united front with the Communists to fight Japan.

That galvanized Vancouver's Chinese-Canadian community into a flurry of fundraising activities. In September of 1937, immediately after the outbreak of the Sino-Japanese war, they raised fifty-five thousand dollars for the Chinese National War Fund. Another major event was the One Bowl of Rice Carnival, sponsored by the Chinese War Refugees Committee. Roughly coinciding with Canada's declaration of war against Germany, the carnival attracted nine thousand visitors and raised twenty-five thousand dollars. Two months later, Chinatown came up with thirty-five hundred dollars for Vancouver's first city-wide War Chest Drive.[40]

Once at war, China appealed to the overseas Chinese for financial help, and the response was overwhelming. In

friends when needed. He describes the different options available in Chinatown of the 1930s:

In the restaurants, there were women from Hong Kong, brought over by businessmen, men who owned grocery stores, labourers. The women lived with these "husbands," but they had been brought over to work, as waitresses and as whores.

The "bachelors" went to the

teahouses to eat, to while away their time, to look at the waitresses. If they saw one they liked, they'd invite her for a late-night snack or something, and then maybe ask her to spend the night with them. The waitresses made good money in those days, twenty to twenty-five dollars a week plus tips. The waitresses didn't have to go with everyone, they could pick and choose only the good-looking

Men sitting at Pender and Carrall, 1936.

Gung Lai Wong of Modernize Tailors and family, 1944. His children included Jack and Bill, who continued the business into the 1980s, Milton K., and Anna, who became a noted artist.

men to go with. Of course, they had to give part of their earnings to their owners.

The men could also go to the brothels. Near Chinatown, there were one or two brothels, owned by Chinese, but all with white girls. They would have three to five women there, you could walk in and choose the girl you wanted and go upstairs. Otherwise, there were three or four white-owned brothels on Hastings Street. And Chinese hotel-keepers could arrange to send a white girl up to your room if you wanted.

Then, there were the white girls working as waitresses in the cafés of Chinatown. They were very friendly, and if you asked them, they might go out with you, for a snack or dinner. And then after a steak dinner, you could ask them to your room. You'd pay two or three dollars or as high as five.

Once there were two men fighting for a waitress. One was a millionaire, the other was just a worker. The worker went out and bought a gun and shot the millionaire on Hastings Street, but only wounded him in the leg. He was sent to jail, and the waitress went with the millionaire.

I often helped the old-timers who got "the dose," or gonorrhea. They had two choices: they could get Chinese herbal tea at thirty-five cents a package, or I could take them to see Dr. Spankey where a shot cost two dollars. A dollar is a day's wages, so a lot of the men took the tea. But some of them came to me complaining, "I've drunk two packages, and I'm still not cured!"

And I would tell them, "It depends on your health. If you're not in good health, then

It was 115 degrees at Poona, India, where the soldiers received further training before heading to fight in Burma and Singapore.

Front, from left: Herbert Lim, Willie Chong; back: Larry Goon, Dick Yip, Bud Quon, Hubie Lee, Gordon Wong.

Vancouver money was raised for military equipment, refugee relief, and aircraft purchases through teas, bazaars, stage shows, parades, and tag days. Chinese war bonds were extensively promoted and sold. In 1942 the Chinese consul urged the community's major soliciting organizations to unify their efforts. Between 1937 and 1945 they sent one million Canadian dollars to China for war aid.[41]

At the same time Chinese Canadians set out to do their fair share in the broader Canadian effort in World War II. In 1941 Vancouver's Chinese pledged to out-subscribe any other Chinese community in Canada on the First Victory Loan Drive. They succeeded in raising half a million dollars, with one in every four Chinese subscribing, compared to the general population's average of one in six in British Columbia and one in eight in Canada.[42]

Chinese-Canadian farmers donated one hundred tons of potatoes to the active service units stationed in Vancouver. When the Red Cross appealed for blood donations, many Chinese responded. They also worked in war industries building ships and aircraft, and in 1941 they formed an Air Raid Patrol of one hundred for Chinatown, and the women formed a platoon in the Ambulance Corps.[43]

When rationing began in 1943, it did not seem to affect Chinese Canadians because they did not consume much black tea, coffee, sugar, or butter. However, the disruptions in shipping caused a jump in imported food prices. Rice and soya sauce went up by 300 per cent, ginger by 1,000 per cent. Other products affected included peanut oil, salt fish, and bean-cakes.[44] When local people attempted to manufacture the goods, they met with limited success.

Chinese Canadians Face the Future

The war focussed attention on one special segment of the community: the new Canadian-borns. This generation had been educated here, many at university, but few could find work outside Chinatown because of racial discrimination. Barred from working in mainstream banks, the government, or any white businesses, the Canadian-borns faced a bleak future. Those taking medical, dental, or other professional degrees looked to China for work. In general, young men went to work in cafés, laundries, or grocery stores. They were waiters, they drove taxis and trucks, they cooked aboard steamships, and they worked in lumberyards. The options for women included cannery work, clerking in grocery stores, or sewing at Charles Chan Kent's garment factory, which was the only operation of its size run by Chinese Canadians.

But while this generation was blocked from working in white Canada, it had ready access to mainstream culture through the education system, the mass media, and the churches. The churches in Chinatown sponsored Young People's Groups, regular meetings, and sports activities. The

the tea doesn't work." And then I would take them to Dr. Spankey. I didn't charge them anything for translating like the other interpreters in Chinatown did. And the men didn't forget. When they got better, and if they won a pot gambling, they would take me out for a steak dinner.

I only know of one or two of the Chinese girls getting the clap. The men would get the clap from the girls they'd pick up off the street or the ones they met at bars. Some men might bring a girl home to the sahn-jai-fong [communal boarding house], where six or seven men lived.

The Experience of Racism

"In those days, no matter how smart, how brilliant you were, you could not get ahead because they would not hire you," dentist William Chu states. "There was no place for a nurse, no place for a pharmacist, no place for a chemical engineer, no place for a doctor, no place for any person of educated capacity."

No matter what direction the Canadian-born Chinese turned in Vancouver in the twenties and thirties, they met racism face to face. Alfred Wong remembers the Alberta Lumber Yard: "I was getting sixty-five cents an hour, good money those days. White guys got about 80 cents, so there was a big difference in wages. But the Chinese figured you were lucky to get a job!"

Some Chinese retreated to Chinatown to make a living. Even there, they had to

Produce trucks and farmers at the open air farmers' wholesale market located near Main and Terminal. At break of dawn, pedlars and greengrocers converged here for the freshest goods.

Roller skating party, 1939. The Canadian-borns had parties, and "everybody came," which meant that everyone was Chinese.

respond creatively to racism. Up to 1940 William Chu says that the Bunn family were the only Chinese mechanics in Chinatown. "They had trained at Vancouver Tech, but nobody would hire them. They usually worked on the Model-T Fords. They had to buy parts, but suppliers wouldn't sell to them. So they bought themselves a lathe and made the parts. If they didn't have gears, they made gears. Or they cut a part up to make something to do the job properly."

Canadian-born Chinese went on to university, but with reduced expectations. Former engineering students Bill and Jack Wong recall: "We were just aiming for a passing mark because we realized we wouldn't be using our education too much. During the final year, we invited the city engineer to talk on oppor-tunities at city hall. He told my class president to tell me not to bother applying because he didn't want to be embarrassed. In other words, they didn't hire Chinese. My class president felt quite bad about it because he didn't realize things were so bad. He was quite surprised that I didn't take it too bad. We knew all along."

These experiences shaped the psychology and outlook of an entire generation. Bill Wong: "You're brought up kind of brainwashed. You accept that you're not expected to feel completely equal. For instance, the Chinese were barred from swimming in a public pool like Crystal Pool. But we were still able to go to UBC and we were able to go to Crystal Pool after hours because a Catholic priest got us in. Well, to us, that's a big privilege. You think you're lucky! Leave well enough

Publication cover from Vancouver's "Oppose Japan and Save China Association," 1933.

Chinese Youth Association organized roller-skating parties, annual picnics on Bowen Island, and Christmas dances. The Chinese Tennis Club built its own clubhouse and courts in the heart of Chinatown. This was a generation caught between two worlds. On one side there was Chinese school, China, and the second-class status of the Chinese in Canada. On the other, there was Canada with its promises of British justice and fair play.

Initially, the Canadian government had decided not to draft Chinese Canadians into the active service. British Columbia politicians had complained that the Asians would claim the right to vote if allowed to bear arms. Legally, no Chinese could vote provincially or federally, and Vancouver's own charter excluded Chinese from civic elections.

However, Chinese-Canadian volunteers joined the services on their own, while the University of British Columbia included Chinese-Canadian students in its Officer Training Corps.

In the summer of 1944 Chinese Canadians were drafted, because by then the Mobilization Board in Vancouver desperately needed men and because war workers complained of being drafted while Chinese Canadians were not. At this point, Chinese Canadians who wanted to serve were applying to leave Canada to join the American armed forces.[45]

Two responses to the call-up surfaced temporarily in the community: one was "No vote, no fight" and the other was "Fight now, vote later." One side felt that since Canada had never treated Chinese Canadians as Canadians, why should they fight? They said, "Give us the franchise first, then we'll go."

The other side argued for enlistment now so that Chinese Canadians could demand the franchise when they returned. The men eventually accepted the draft and the majority volunteered to go overseas. They were integrated in basic training with other Canadians, and special camps were

alone, why rock the boat?"

Ultimately, Canadian-born Chinese were optimistic because they saw things changing. Jack Wong: "At school, they taught us about democracy and equal rights. And the way we were brought up at the church, you could see that eventually things would be equal. So there wasn't a need for raising hell. We felt we just had to be patient."

Off to War

World War II forced young Chinese Canadians to make tough decisions despite Canadian racism to participate in the country's war effort. Before Chinese Canadians were drafted, Alfred Wong tried to enlist in the Navy: "I filled in an application and I asked them a whole pile of things. They said, 'We might accept you, and if we do, you have the shore job.' I said,

F.O. QUON LOUIE, R.C.A.F.

Quon Louie was a cleancut young Chinese athlete, adept at tennis, basketball and soccer. Being an active member of our club for many years, he possesses the quality of a true sportsman and believes in the spirit of fair play.

Early in the war he enlisted in the R.C.A.F. He became a flying officer and one of the few Chinese bombardiers in the service. In January of 1944, when Quon was 24, his flak-riddled plane cascaded down in flames on German soil. Later the R.C.A.F. announced that F.O. Quon Louie had been officially presumed dead.

We extend our condolences and sympathy, while at the same time we feel great pride in the glory that our heroes have won.

F.O. Quon Louie   GOD BLESS HIM

Obituary for Flying Officer Quon Louie, a member of Vancouver's prominent H. Y. Louie family. From the *Chinese Tennis Club Annual*, 1946

'What's that?' And they answered, 'Naturally, your job is a cook.'"

William Chu, a dental student in 1942, refused to join the Officer Training Corps, and the dean called him down. "'I notice that you refuse to join,' he said. 'We are fighting for the British Empire, we are fighting for our queen and king and all our freedom in Canada.'

"I said, 'I am not even a Canadian, I am a Chinese. If I go to Seattle, I have to go to the Chinese consul to get a visa to go. We have no rights in British Columbia. We cannot practise law, we cannot open a drugstore, we cannot teach in school, we cannot work in the post office, we have no rights.' He let the matter drop."

But when the draft came, Chinese Canadians went readily, and though not required to do so, most volunteered for overseas service.

After basic training in Chilliwack, the men went to India via England for further instruction. Robert Chan Kent: "The second phase of training included dynamite, wireless, physical, and parachute training. We were supposed to fly behind the enemy line, drop by parachute, establish camp, and sabotage their railway and lines of communication."

This behind-the-line combat had its own special risks, as Sergeant Roy Mah recalls, "We weren't fighting frontal warfare, which involves a number of divisions and companies. Instead, we were intelligence units operating in groups of six. I tell you, I was scared! I'm no hero, I don't mind admitting it. Tossing you behind enemy lines, who wouldn't be scared? You have a fifty-fifty chance of coming back. Once you're in there, you can't get out. We were well

Wing Wong at Buna Beach, New Guinea, 1944. Wong was also sent to Sumatra, Singapore, and Hong Kong to train the local underground in resistance work.

established only for secret training. At Okanagan Lake, members of Secret Force 136 learned demolition and commando techniques before going to Asia for sabotage and reconnaissance work behind Japanese lines.

The war efforts of the Chinese-Canadian community gave it an unprecedented positive public image in the press. China was an ally of Canada, and Chinese Canadians were seen fighting two wars: Canada's and China's. In 1943 a dominion-wide Aid to China Fund was launched by prominent whites to relieve starvation in China. The fund was supported by local Chinese Canadians and raised $1,250,000 all across Canada.[46] There were fundraising banquets such as that held at the Hotel Vancouver in June 1944 by the Chinese War Relief Committee, attended by the lieutenant-governor and prominent leaders from military and civilian life.[47] There was also favourable press coverage of visitors from China such as scholars, air pilots, and artists.

In the postwar years, public opinion in Canada swung over to the side of the Chinese Canadians. The 1923 exclusion act was repealed in May of 1947, but only dependants of Canadian citizens were allowed in. In the spring 1947 session of the British Columbia legislature, the elections act was amended to give the vote to Chinese Canadians. Once on the provincial voters list, they could vote in federal elections, too.

equipped: fish-hooks, mosquito nets, rifles and even cyanide pills. We were told, 'If you're caught, just take one. Don't talk, just swallow the pill.'"

But before all the Chinese Canadians could be deployed, peace came. Herbert Lim: "We were all set to go. Most of us had made four practice jumps, and two days more would have seen us in action. I think many of the boys were disappointed

when the enemy did quit."

Three Vancouver soldiers, Sgt. Norman Low, Sgt. Louey King, and Sgt. James Shiu were awarded the Military Medal in 1946. Low's official citation read:

Norman Low was parachuted into the Rejang River district of Sarawak, Borneo, deep in enemy territory. There he organized communications for patrols which gave field headquarters

Roy Mah, 1987.

vital information. With utter disregard for his own safety he maintained his wireless link inside the enemy's area, frequently passing out intelligence under direct enemy attack. His coolness and bravery, his resourcefulness and initiative played a significant part in the success of the Rejang River operations.

Won Alexander Cumyow casting a ballot, 1949. When the provincial government finally allowed the Chinese to vote in 1947, that qualified them to vote in federal elections too.

DOMINION OF

Postwar Changes: Immigration and Acceptance

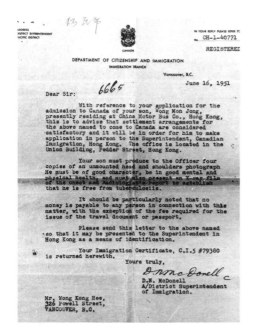

Letter, 1951. An eagerly awaited letter that notified Chinese Canadians that family members would be allowed into Canada.

When World War II ended and Pacific shipping resumed, many Chinese old-timers headed for China. In three months in 1946, $1.5 million was converted into Hong Kong currency when they sold business and real estate holdings here.[1] By year's end, some fifteen hundred Chinese had left to board ships in San Francisco.[2] Some were heading to see their homeland for the last time; in fact, several who had bought tickets and packed their bags died before their group could leave. It was commonly noted at the time that "Chinese are like B.C. salmon. When they die, they like to be in the place where they were born."

The "bachelors" who chose not to go back tried instead to bring their families over, but obstacles remained. Although the 1923 exclusion law was repealed in 1947, federal Order in Council P.C. 2115 still restricted Chinese immigration to Canada. This 1930 regulation allowed only the wives of Canadian citizens and their children under eighteen to enter Canada from China. The unfairness was obvious, because Canada was accepting large numbers of refugees and immigrants from postwar Europe who had no family ties here. Other Canadian immigrants who had only resident status could send for their relatives. Clearly, Canada was reluctant to accept the Chinese. Prime Minister Mackenzie King stated in 1947:

The policy of the government is to foster the growth of the population of Canada by the encouragement of immigration. . . . The essential thing is that immigrants be selected with care, and that their numbers be adjusted to the absorptive capacity of the country.

There will, I am sure, be general agreement with the view that the people of Canada do not wish, as a result of mass immigration, to make a funda- mental alteration in the character of our population. Large-scale immigration from the Orient would change that fundamental composition of the Canadian population.[3]

In other words, the government wanted new immigrants, but preferably white ones. Between 1947 and 1954, eleven thousand Chinese came to Canada, less than one per cent of the overall immigration of 1.15 million. Still, P.C. 2115 was not repealed until 1956, and Foon Sien, president of the Vancouver Chinese Benevolent Association, made annual treks to Ottawa to lobby for amendments. Changes·were granted in piecemeal fashion. The age of admissible children was raised to nineteen in 1949 and to twenty-one in 1950. In 1951 Chinese-Canadian women could bring in husbands, just as men brought in wives. In 1954 naturalization rules were relaxed, and a year later the age limit of admissible children was boosted to twenty-five. Foon Sien stated the Chinese position over and over:

Tears have been dropped on every page of Chinese immigration history in

Changes in public attitudes towards the Chinese finally permitted this man to acquire Canadian citizenship in 1963 after years of systemic exclusion. In previous years, the courts could grant citizenship to aliens, but judges rarely did so for the Chinese.

Canada. They have suffered as no other racial group or nationality. They were singled out to be discriminated against, and yet they harbor no animosity. They continue to plead for their cause, hoping that one day the authorities will see their point of view and accord them the same privileges and rights as other Canadians enjoy.

What we ask is not an open door to all Chinese who wish to come. Our appeal is that the Chinese Canadian may have his family with him—a complete family, not one part in Canada and the other part in Hong Kong or China.[4]

The Booming Fifties

Between 1951 and 1961, Vancouver's Chinese population doubled from 8,729 to 15,223. The wives and children of long-separated families were arriving and the birth rate was climbing. A Chinese-Canadian newspaper remarked in 1950 that Chinese weddings happened every week in town! As well, Chinese from elsewhere in Canada, especially

---

That Guy Is a Commie

When China came under Communist rule in 1949, the lives of Chinese Canadians were profoundly affected, although each generation felt the impact differently.

Old-timers

M. SETO: *In 1949 my wife sent a letter and asked for money to buy some land. I sent over a thousand dollars Canadian, and she bought the land. But two months later the Communists came and took my land. They took it all! Other people may have gold and savings, but not me. I had nothing left. That was all of my savings. And they tore down my house. Why did they do that?*

Wives

MRS. F. G. LEE: *My husband brought my son over first, that was easy. But when my husband applied for me, the authorities wouldn't let me out. They wanted me there so that my husband would keep sending money back. They needed the foreign currency.*

Canadian-borns

IAN LEE: *The white community looked upon Red China as this great massive evil giant, and the Chinese in Vancouver saw that they had to look at it in the same way,* just to prove themselves. When the Korean War came along, local Chinese put themselves as far away from the conflict as they possibly could. There was no compassion for the regime in China, there was no understanding, not even an attempt to want to have anything to do with it. They were looked upon as the enemy.

ANDREW JOE: *A lot of people didn't know what was going*

Street vendor selling fresh crabs to passers-by on Pender Street, 1960.

Vancouver Island and the prairies, were moving to Vancouver.

The New Chinatown

In the 1950s the look of Chinatown changed. Several of the large old buildings at the western edge of Chinatown were destroyed, but elsewhere on Pender Street business boomed. Several new Chinese supermarkets and restaurants opened, including a drive-in eatery. Goods never before sold in Chinatown appeared: televisions, furniture, and major appliances. There was a Chinese driving school and a Chinese brokerage house. By 1956 Chinatown had seven nightclubs, more per square block than any other part of town. Chinese movies were shown every week at the Avon starting in 1958. Several realty, insurance, and finance companies run by young Chinese Canadians started up. Older firms remodelled and expanded.

In 1949 one quarter of Vancouver's Chinese lived outside Chinatown, but there were still neighbourhoods where

Andrew Joe, 1987.

on. With McCarthyism, a lot of people were afraid to find out. Even in Chinatown, people were afraid to read books on China or listen to speakers. If you owned a Paul Robeson record, the RCMP were liable to come around. People who read or subscribed to Chinese magazines like China Reconstructs or Peking Review would get a knock on the door from the RCMP. And if they didn't get intimidated, then the

RCMP tried to intimidate their employers by saying, "Hey, you know that guy who works for you? That guy is a Commie!"

New Immigrant Youth
VICTOR LEE: *The new immigrants, especially the teenagers, were quite nationalistic. They had suffered through the Japanese invasion and they knew from history how China had suffered. They*

wanted China to be strong and prosperous. Then, because of their limited knowledge of the Canadian scene and language, they read the Chinese news, so their orientation and identification was still with China. They did not necessarily agree with the Communist ideology, but they were proud.

The older generation's dream was to go back and buy land and live off the land, collecting rent. Their hopes

Cartoon "University of Democracy."
From *New Citizen*, 1949

GRADUATION

A Chinese chess tournament sponsored by
Hon Hsing and Hai Fung ran for two weeks
in 1961.

were dashed by the revolution so naturally they were hostile to the new China. The older generation didn't think that things there were serious. They thought that it was temporary and that they would go back someday. The younger generation realized after a while that they were going to set their roots here and shifted their orientation from China to Canada, but the transition took a while.

"Leftist" Organizations

JIMMY LUM: *The Chinese Youth Association was seen as being left wing. We showed films from the Peace Council, which was part of the very strong left movement here then. We borrowed films from China, too. The first one we had was called* On the Huai River Flowers Grow on Both Banks. *We were showing it in the Pender Auditorium, and the authorities came along and confiscated it. And someone broke into the* CYA *and burned the library and wrecked the darkroom. People thought we had connections to China, but we were just a bunch of young people hanging around together.*

Were we scared? Just a little. Our parents threatened to disown us. We weren't afraid. When you're young, what are you afraid of? You have a totally different outlook. But other people were afraid, they didn't want to come near us!

No Matter How Hard...

In the 1950s several issues confronted Canadian-born Chinese. The racial climate was improving, but awkward moments cropped up as this young generation groped for new manners appropriate to the changing times. They celebrated newly won rights and privileges, but visibility remained an issue.

The New Citizen was an English-language Chinese-Canadian newspaper that started in 1949. That year it noted: "The Chinese-Canadian youth has a duty and a responsibility to Canada, this land of our birth. Technically, legally, and in every respect he is a Canadian, but no matter how hard he attempts to pretend he is a Canadian, fellow Canadians will look upon him as Chinese."

Caught between idealistic dreams and the everyday reality of race relations, Canadian-borns moved cautiously into the mainstream. "It was odd, in a way. They'd move away from Chinatown, but never really move away," comments Ian Lee, who was born in 1938. "At school, they were really friendly and outgoing and they made friends with the whites. But then they'd go back to Pender Street, to the Pender Y, where they'd hang around with all their real friends.

"On campus, everybody belonged to the Chinese Varsity Club, and that was a Canadian Chinese club, as opposed to the Hong Kong Chinese. The native-borns socialized together, studied together, they did everything together. But they weren't

Wong Mow, Chinatown tailor, at work in 1960. Wong, who had long specialized in shirt-making, soon realized he could not compete with permanent-press shirts. His Canadian-born sons went on to university and did not enter the family trade.

Asians could not buy property. A "Chinese Shaughnessy" had sprung up in the South Cambie area near Twenty-fifth Avenue, where thirty wealthy Chinese families lived.[5] In the 1950s population growth was so great that even though more and more Chinese moved away from Chinatown, Strathcona's Chinese component increased steadily. Many new immigrant families chose to live there because it was comfortingly close to Chinatown, which remained the focal point of the community.

Two local Chinese firms expanded into non-Chinese markets at this time. The H. Y. Louie Company opened a forty-thousand-square-foot office-warehouse in 1954 and acquired IGA's British Columbia franchise in 1955. In ten years' time the company was wholesaler to some forty-seven IGA supermarkets. Charles Chan Kent's C. Kent & Company and his Vancouver Shirt and Overall Manufacturing Company became Aero Garment Limited in 1952 and began to market

Chinese Lumber Worker, a union-sponsored newspaper used to organize Chinese workers in the industry.

Donna Chan, 1987.

interested in the politics of the country at that time. They were interested in being accepted and becoming part of the community, but not in being catalysts to create a new situation."

Donna Chan, another teenager in the 1950s, recalls how important Chinatown was: "The parents thought it was wonderful that their daughters could come back to Chinatown to meet other Chinese girls in the drill team. There was a feeling of belonging. It was hard to feel that you really belonged somewhere because you felt different and the prejudice was still there. So here you could relax because you were among your own."

The feelings of caution and the need for comfort were natural responses to the bewildering changes occurring rapidly around them. But they were counterbalanced by lofty ambitions. *The New Citizen* reminded Canadian-borns to remember their community: "On the social level we must demonstrate our adaptability to Canadian ways and broaden our social contacts. Each and every one of us must put forth his maximum effort in his work. Each of us represents not only himself but all Chinese Canadians. Let us be worthy of the group."

Harvey K. Lowe, the first Chinese-Canadian radio announcer, 1951.

Lim D. Lee, the first Chinese-Canadian pharmacist to own a drugstore, 1951.

The First Chinese-Canadian Pharmacist

Pharmacy was one profession that admitted only those people who were qualified to vote in B.C. Since Chinese Canadians were disenfranchised in this province, they could not become pharmacists until after 1947. Within a month of his graduation in 1951, Lim Lee became the first Chinese Canadian to own and operate a pharmacy in Canada.

When I first started, I only had a small place at 444 Main Street, and it was as good as it could be under the circumstances. It was just like another drugstore, only smaller. At the beginning, my customers who couldn't speak English would bring in a bottle not dispensed in my store and ask me how to take it and what it was for. It was like going into a restaurant and ordering food and then going across the street to another restaurant to ask for salt and pepper to use. It was funny, but I never offended them. Slowly and gradually they patronized me.

Some of them would bring me some pill that was dispensed twenty years ago and say, "I want some more of those pills, they were red and pink and long." That was so ridiculous, I couldn't take a chance even if I knew.

I got to know most of the older people because they needed Chinese interpretations of what they were taking. I also made appointments with doctors and I got them taxis.

nationally. He built a hundred-thousand-square-foot factory not far from Chinatown in 1958 and became one of the first to manufacture permanent-press clothing in Canada.

Across Canada the economy was booming and wages were improving. In the lumber and fish-canning industries the contract labour system was ousted when unions started organizing Chinese labourers. Lumber workers who once received a dollar a day now earned a dollar an hour.[6] Organized labour advocated equal treatment of Chinese workers and set up a Joint Labour Committee to Combat Racial Discrimination in 1951.[7] The thousand-member Chinese Trade Workers Association, an organization of hotel and restaurant workers, launched a membership drive in 1948 to increase membership to ten thousand and to affiliate with the B.C. Trades and Labour Council.[8] Throughout this period, Chinese Canadians continued to work where white Canada had allowed them: in restaurants, laundries, grocery stores, rooming houses, farms, shingle mills, and wholesale houses.

At the same time a new generation of English-speaking and mostly Canadian-born professionals was emerging. Professional associations gradually began to admit Chinese-Canadian members. The first Chinese notary publics in British Columbia, Gordon Cumyow and Quon H. Wong, were appointed in 1950, but the notarial association restricted their practices to the Chinatown area.[9] This was the beginning of a proud procession of Chinese-Canadian firsts. The University of British Columbia admitted its first Chinese-Canadian medical student, Eddy Fung, and pharmacist Lim Lee opened the first drugstore in Chinatown in 1951. City hall hired its first Chinese-Canadian employee, Jessie Lee, in 1952. A year later Andrew Joe was the first Chinese lawyer admitted to the bar, Diana Lam was the first Chinese-Canadian admitted to a sorority, and the first all-Chinese Lions Club in Canada was formed. The year 1954 saw the admission of the first Chinese-Canadian woman lawyer and the first two Chinese-Canadian chartered accountants. Lawyer Douglas Jung was the first Chinese Canadian elected to Parliament, representing Vancouver Centre in 1957. In 1959 Tim Louie became the first Chinese Canadian to sit on the directorate of the Vancouver Board of Trade.

A New Generation of Immigrants

The youthful newcomers of the 1950s were distinctly different from the established Chinese Canadians, and their differences often fostered conflict. Most of them could not speak English and were still required to remit earnings to families in China. Many were idealistic: they had left a China still struggling to modernize and to recover from the destruction of World War II, and they wanted to acquire an education and return to help national reconstruction. They were often more sophisticated than earlier generations of

Harvey Lowe

Harvey Lowe, who first made his reputation as a boy-wonder world yo-yo champion, started broadcasting "The Call of China" in 1951 on Vancouver's CJOR radio. It was the first Chinese-Canadian radio program and ran for fourteen years. Below are excerpts from an interview with Harvey Lowe by Howard Yan and Jim Wong-Chu, published in the UBC Chinese Students' Association *Journal* in 1985.

When I came back from China in the summer of 1949 I had a hard time looking for work. I took a few of the clips I had made at home to a few radio stations, and they were willing to listen to them. I went into CJOR and met a man called Jack Short, "the voice of the races." He was very enthusiastic about "The Call of China" and helped me get a program going.

In the beginning I had to work very hard, writing the program and selling it to commercial sponsors. Later on, the Bamboo Terrace took me on and sponsored me for eleven and a half years.

The show was broadcast in English every Sunday afternoon from two to two-thirty. We tried to deal with everything authentically Chinese. I might be talking about pagodas, and I'd do research on that. Between each segment, I'd play a lot of Chinese music. There were more Canadian listeners than Chinese because the program was directed more toward them.

I had planned for a Chinese program, but if a station injected a Chinese program with Chinese dialogue into their English schedule, they'd lose all of their audience.[24]

View of Chinatown's neon signs at night, 1960. Pender Street's colours were featured on many post cards.

Remembering Chinatown

Larry Wong worked for the *Chinatown News* during the 1950s. He recalls:

In the 1950s Chinatown was so small everyone knew one another. You could walk down the street and see elderly Chinese standing on the street, talking to each other and enjoying the sun. There was no real hustle and bustle, but they knew who the young ones were and who the new arrivals were. There was a closeness in Chinatown — you really knew your neighbours.

Chinatown's reputation was sleazy. Pender Street was close to Hastings with its dope addicts and prostitutes, so you associated Chinatown with those elements. At the corner of Pender and Main was a nightclub called the Kubla Khan. They had loud music and attracted the wrong type of people. Further down on Main Street was another club called the New Delhi that played rock and roll really loud.

On any Saturday night, traffic along Pender and Main was bumper to bumper, with people having a good time and getting drunk. It was an invasion, because during the day Chinatown was busy but subdued and minding its own business. But at night, these noisy elements came down and treated Chinatown like a playground.

Most of my friends were moving away from Chinatown. I think the fact that everyone knew one another in Chinatown was uncomfortable for some, so they had to get away. But there was comfort and security in the village quality of Chinatown. Some people might call it a ghetto, but I wouldn't.

Every Hallowe'en the white gangs would go down to

Bamboo Terrace Restaurant, 1960. This was the first restaurant in Chinatown to install air conditioning.

Chinatown and line up on either side of the street and throw firecrackers and roman candles at each other. It was really fierce and people hurt themselves. The streets were full of litter, there was a heavy smell of gunpowder, and someone would smear the windows of the stores. It was a real mess. Chinatown was treated like a mat for wiping your feet, for cleaning your shoes.

Men waiting outside Pender Street gambling halls as civic officials tour through them. In 1949 the first club licence was issued to a Chinese club. The police chief opposed this, saying that it legalized gambling. The tour let officials see that the clubs primarily served pleasure and leisure functions.

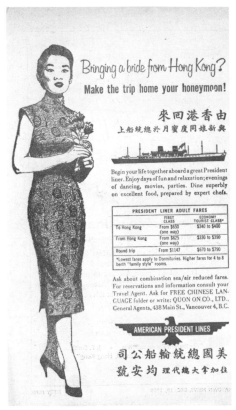

"Bringing a Bride from Hong Kong?"
From *Chinatown*, c. 1957

immigrants; the newcomers had often attended schools in county towns where Western content was taught, and had often spent time in Hong Kong where they became Westernized, especially with spending money received from Canada.

More sons came because sponsoring fathers thought males could earn more. When the young men arrived they attended New Canadian classes in the public schools before being streamed into regular classes. Others went to work and, because of language limitations, often followed their fathers into manual labour in mills and in restaurants. Working in Chinatown or with Chinese crews slowed the process of learning English, so the churches of Chinatown quickly set up night classes for them. A small number continued on to university, while others went into the small towns of British Columbia to work.

These newcomers sparked strong reactions from the existing Chinese-Canadian community. Fathers who had earned pittance wages when they first arrived were outraged to see their sons spending money freely on cars, cameras, fountain pens, and tennis rackets,[10] and complained about the lack of respect they received. The new immigrants and their Canadian-born counterparts hardly mixed because interests, occupations, and cultural backgrounds were quite different. In fact, Canadian-borns were often hostile to people from the Old Country. In one instance, a snowball fight between teenagers of the two groups grew into a pitched battle so fierce that the police were summoned.

The young men were soon of marriageable age, but the ratio of men to women in Chinatown was about three-to-one because sponsoring fathers had not brought over daughters of the same generation. Many men went back to Hong Kong to marry and applied for their wives to join them. In August of 1956 immigration regulations were relaxed to allow them to send for prospective brides upon paying a

---

In the old days, the vendors were out there on the sidewalk, with live chickens in cages so you had all the smells and the screaming. One old man used to carry a battered suitcase to the nightclubs and open it to show orchids, roses, and gardenias, and say, "You likee nice flowers?"

New Immigrants: Wives
"Why did I want to come over?" Mrs. Git Fong Louie sits in her Strathcona apartment and chuckles at a seemingly silly question. "Everyone was coming over, so of course I wanted to come. Times were tough at home. After Liberation, there were food shortages: you couldn't buy fish or shrimp or pork. There were long line-ups. Even if you had money you couldn't buy

the food you needed."
Mrs. Louie was one of the wives of the "bachelors" who had worked for decades in Canada without their families. When these wives were finally allowed to join their husbands in the 1950s, they faced the culture shock of Canada (especially harsh if they had come straight from the village) as well as the old-fashioned responses of their own men.
Mrs. Lee Woo arrived in

Mrs. M.L. Jung, 1987.

A New Canadian class at Lord Strathcona School, 1961. These classes emphasized learning English-language skills. Other new immigrants who worked during the day attended tutored classes available near Chinatown.

1950 without any knowledge of English or any friends. "I went to Woodward's Department Store alone and they all said I was brave. They said, 'That woman doesn't speak a word of English, yet she goes to town all the time.'

"It was very old-fashioned before," she continues. "If you stared out the window, people would say, 'So-and-so's wife has no shame.' When I walked in Chinatown when I first came here, the local Chinese men stopped and stared. They hadn't seen a woman on the streets much."

Their husbands' income determined whether these women worked or not. Mrs. M. L. Jung came in 1950 at age fifty. "I hadn't seen my husband for twenty-three years, so of course I wanted to come. We had no children, so I came alone. My husband had a grocery store downtown on Granville Street, but I didn't have to work because he had partners."

So she stayed home. "All the neighbours were Westerners, but I didn't know English so I couldn't talk to them. There were no English classes around, so I learned a bit from my neighbour. She might invite me over for tea and point out 'cup' or 'saucer' and words like that. And I learned to count in English.

"Usually I sat all day in the kitchen with the stove. Or I planted flowers, raked leaves, or mowed the lawn. Slowly I learned to ride the streetcars, but I only went to Chinatown. Fortunately there was church. I was a Christian in Hong Kong so both my husband and I attended the Chinese United Church."

For those women who went to work, there were only hard, menial jobs. Mrs. Lee Woo: "I

Chinese Freemasons lead a parade down
Pender Street, 1964. They brought the first
dragon to Vancouver's Chinatown.

POSTWAR CHANGES

121

thousand-dollar deposit bond. The new-immigrant population thus began to increase more rapidly than the Canadian-born.

Many new immigrants joined long-standing Chinatown organizations such as the Freemasons or the Hon Hsing Athletic Club, which fostered aspects of traditional culture. But new clubs also emerged that offered contemporary Western forms of recreation. One of these was the Hai Fung Club, formed in 1957. Its membership was young and largely student, but also included workers and other professionals. They set up a library, gym, and darkroom and organized ping-pong, chess, and volleyball tournaments, a speech contest, and exhibits of local art.

A New Era of Assimilation

The 1950s offered great promise to Vancouver's Chinese Canadians. Discriminatory laws were repealed, Canada signed the United Nations Charter with its affirmation of human rights, and local newspapers railed against any overt acts of racism. There was greater mobility and there were more opportunities. But total acceptance did not occur overnight.

Chinatown worked hard to present its best possible side. The Chinese-Canadian war veterans raised ten thousand dollars to send comfort parcels to Canadian troops fighting in Korea. The Chinatown Lions Club donated to crippled children and medical research. The Chinese Benevolent Association endorsed campaigns for the Red Cross, for the 1948 Fraser River flood relief, and for the Children's Hospital. Starting in 1954 the Pender Y organized well-attended Chinatown tours to introduce curious outsiders to the community. The newly formed Vancouver Chinese Chamber of Commerce, which included prominent businessmen such as Charles Chan Kent and Tim Louie, sponsored a four-day festival for the 1959 Chinese New Year, the first such organized celebration.

Increasingly, Canadian-born Chinese turned away from things

In 1963 when the Hon Hsing Athletic Club celebrated its twenty-third anniversary with a lion parade and street performance of martial arts, it drew enormous crowds.

didn't have a cent when I first came. My husband was penniless, he couldn't find a job. I wanted to buy a sewing machine, to alter clothes, to mend things. But it cost $220, so I made monthly payments. I had three jobs. I worked in the fish cannery, I gathered seeds, and I peeled shrimps."

Mrs. Git Fong Louie: "It was hard to find work. They hired the younger women but not us. I went potato picking and strawberry picking. The truck they used to carry us to the farm was an old, beat-up thing. There were two rows of wooden seats on the back, and ropes and potato sacks tied around the sides. You had to climb on, and if you weren't careful, you could fall off. They were like the trucks used for hauling pigs to Macao! My husband didn't want me working in the fields, but I went anyway."

New Arrivals: Sons
"Back in China, they used to be the richest kid in the village. But over here, they had to work and all they got were lousy jobs. They were really frustrated. One fellow killed himself: he went home and slit his wrists."

Jimmy Lum, who arrived in Canada in 1950 at age fourteen, is describing his generation of young newcomers. They were the China-born sons of the old-timers who had become Canadian citizens and sponsored their offspring over. Most of these were teenagers and young men when they arrived.

Typically, they attended New Canadian classes before being streamed into the regular school system. They struggled with the English language. Victor Lee, who also arrived in 1950 at age fourteen, recalls,

Kindergarten graduation at the Chinese United Church, 1962. Many of these students were born of new immigrant parents. The children not wearing gowns and mortarboards were next year's graduates.

The north side of the 200-block East Pender held at least four live poultry shops. Up until 1966 a customer could walk into a store, select a live bird, and wait while it was killed and dressed.

"Conversational English they could take up, but when they got to high school and had to study Shakespearean plays and Victorian English, they would have problems."

Economic pressures also weighed on the newcomers. Victor Lee went to work after a year and a half at Strathcona Primary School. "I washed dishes for four years. I had a mother to support in China, I had borrowed money for the fees to come over, and had to pay for my year and a half of education and living expenses."

The future looked grim for this generation. Their economic resources were poor and their English fluency was not good. Jimmy Lum: "They knew they were intellectually capable, but they couldn't break through, they couldn't get the jobs they wanted. There was nothing they could do. They wanted to learn, to get ahead, but still they had to support themselves. Yet they could barely make a living."

Their frustrations were magnified by their own idealism. They were young and bright, they watched China emerge from years of war, they yearned to help rebuild the country, and all around them the postwar economy was booming. Victor Lee: "I was dreaming of becoming a scientist, mainly because science wasn't developed in China. That was my dream, but reality is a different thing. My first job was working on the CPR ships going between Seattle, Vancouver, and Nanaimo, and I used to sit beside the rail and look at the sea gulls and the sunset and

feel depressed."

Ultimately, there were stories of both success and failure. Victor Lee finished high school at night and through correspondence school and went on to study engineering at university. He notes, "Unless you had a good education, you could not break out of Chinatown."

Jimmy Lum: "One or two got so frustrated they went a little crazy. You saw them wandering along the street, mumbling or singing to themselves. They were working, sure, but they were in bad shape. People in Chinatown said, 'The young people are useless, they don't listen, they're lazy.'"

One final frustration was the lack of girls because the old-timers had brought over mostly sons. Victor Lee chuckles, "They used to say there were no ugly girls in Chinatown!"

I Was an Illegal Immigrant

In the 1950s, Chinese-Canadian citizens could sponsor only their children or wives as immigrants to Canada. They could not bring over grandchildren, parents, siblings, or any other relatives. "Paper families" that could claim sons or daughters from China were used to help nonadmissible people enter. Lee Kwan Tai (a pseudonym) was one of them. He told his story to Robert McKeown of *Weekend Magazine*, which published it in April 1961.

I was living in my village in Toy Shan when the Communists took over China in 1949. My father had died in the Japanese war, and my mother looked after my brother and

View of the north side of Pender Street, 1961. Notice the fleet of taxicabs. Chinatown once had several of its own taxi companies.

me. We were very poor, and my grandfather, who had lived in Vancouver since about 1910, had helped us for many years by sending money.

Now my grandfather wrote that I must go to Hong Kong. He said that if I went there I might have a chance of getting to Canada. Some clan cousins of ours from the next village had a shop in Hong Kong and I went to live with them. I lived there for about three years. My grandfather sent them money for my board but I also helped in the shop. I went to night school to study English and in the daytime I went to accounting school.

A friend I made told me that he knew someone who had papers to sell that would get me to Canada. I sent a letter to my grandfather in Vancouver and asked if he was willing to buy the paper for me and he said he was.

The man said we would have to pay five hundred dollars down and another five hundred dollars when I passed the examination and got my passport. The rest would be paid after I arrived in Canada.

The man gave me a coaching paper. This was a paper telling all about who I was supposed to be. The man said I had one month to learn it. The coaching paper told everything about my paper family—names, ages, where we had lived and gone to school, who the teachers were, and everything that was important about the village where they lived. . . .

I got another letter and went to the Canadian immigration office again. This time I was called to a different desk where a Chinese man questioned me. This time was different. This time it was really tough.

He asked me questions for four and a half hours. He was trying to get me to give a wrong answer and show I was not really the son of the man in Ontario.

"You are too old," he said. "You are not eighteen years old."

"Yes, I am," I said. "You are wrong."

"You are not Toy Shanese people," he said. "You do not speak like Toy Shanese people. You speak like you are from a different district."

He showed me some pictures of people from the same village as my paper family—about two dozen pictures. He told me every one of them was from the same village and said I should pick out the ones I knew. I picked out my paper father and mother and two other people from the village. I said, "That is all I know. The rest I don't know."

"They are all from that village," he said. "You should know all of them."

When I left the office, the last thing he said was, "You are not going to Canada."

I was very sad when I went home. I was hopeless. I went to see the agent who had given me the coaching paper and told him what had happened.

"You must have made a mistake," he said. "You must have said something wrong."

One day next March a letter came from the immigration office telling me to come for a medical check-up. I was so happy. How could it be that after so long I was really going

Chinese. Despite rising enrolments in Chinese-language schools in the early 1950s, Canadian-born attendance soon dropped. The reasons varied: some parents felt that Chinese school was a stumbling block to assimilation and preferred their children to take piano or dance lessons;[11] most Canadian-born families lived outside Chinatown, where the schools were located; the children themselves were not keen to attend, and the need to use Chinese at work had dropped greatly. Canadian-born disinterest was also blamed for the lack of Chinese New Year celebrations in Chinatown in the early 1960s.

Two Chinas

Current events in China created new tensions in the community. When World War II ended, the Communists under Mao Zedong and Nationalists under Chiang Kai-shek continued to fight a civil war in China that finally ended in 1949 with a Communist victory. The incompetence and corruption of the Nationalists, or Kuomintang, had cost them popular support, and they fled to the island of Taiwan to set up their own government. The United States quickly became blatantly hostile to the People's Republic of China because of fears of a worldwide Communist takeover, and accordingly, Taiwan, not mainland China, was given a seat in the United Nations.

In Vancouver the Chinese dutifully followed Canada's recognition of the Nationalist government, and the Chinese Benevolent Association sent a letter of support to Taiwan in 1949.[12] The correct line to follow then was to be pro-Taiwan; anything else was construed as "red."

But community opinion was not united. The Chinese Freemasons formed an Anti-Totalitarian Society, which pledged to resist *all* forms of dictatorship, including the one on Taiwan. They had declared their neutrality in China's politics during the Chinese civil war and maintained an anti-Kuomintang yet non-pro- Communist position afterwards. And two new independent Chinese language dailies were launched in 1953 to reflect still other political viewpoints in the community.

Nevertheless, Taiwan's influence was strong in Vancouver. The Nationalist consul had offices here and was prominent in the official and social circles of the city. Nationalist holidays were celebrated in Chinatown, and clan and Old Country home-district associations sent funds to the Army Comfort Fund in Taiwan. The Kuomintang was viewed as the staunch defender of Chinese tradition, while the Communists were not. As a result Chinese-Canadian organizations decided in 1951 that 860 sets of human bones awaiting shipment to China since 1939 for reburial would remain here instead.[13] Nationalist supporters took an active anti-Communist position. When multimillion-dollar wheat sales between China and Canada were announced in 1962, local Nationalists picketed the hotel of the officials from China.[14]

---

to go to Canada after all?

I landed in Vancouver in April 1953 and stayed with my grandfather for a week. Then I came to Ontario to live with my paper family, since they believed the immigration people might come to check up on me.

In the past eight years I have worked in restaurants. Sometimes I have had no job. I have also gone to school and learned English. I am working again in a restaurant and sending money to help my family who have got to Hong Kong from Toy Shan.

A few months ago I told the police how I came to Canada. They have not sent me back to Hong Kong but have let me keep on working in Canada. I am very glad to be living in the open once more.[25]

Generation Gaps

The arrival of a new wave of Chinese immigrants, mostly young men, in the 1950s created tension in Chinatown, which had traditionally been dominated by allegiances to Old Country home-district associations, clan surname groups, and political parties. Now a new element came into play when Canadian-born young people treated these newcomers as foreigners.

Larry Wong recalls the atmosphere at Strathcona Primary School: "When immigrants integrated with the regular class, if they were speaking Chinese to each other the teacher would say, 'No, don't speak Chinese here. You are here to learn English.' Of course, we would pick up on that and harp on the New Canadians. And normally when you have a snowball fight, it's all fun. But a few

Refugees from China arriving in Vancouver, 1962. That year, Canada permitted 100 families from China to enter under a refugee sponsorship program.

However, the brouhaha really took place at an official level, where the Nationalists were recognized as the legitimate Chinese government by local community leaders. At a personal level, most Chinese Canadians were not interested in two-China politics, preferring to think of themselves as Canadian first and Chinese second.

Immigration

During this period there were sensationalized newspaper reports of Communist conspiracies in the Chinese community. The *Vancouver Daily Province*'s front-page headline for 8 April 1952, read, "Red Agents Move Freely into B.C." The story charged that 85 per cent of the young Chinese arrivals were pro-Communist and doing leftist organizational work in Chinatown. In the middle of the Korean War such alarming allegations linked the local Chinese to an enemy power. The CBA protested vigorously: "We know of no Red organizers or Communist agents and we repudiate the

times you could see that all the Canadian boys were on one side and the Chinese immigrants were on the other, and we were throwing these snowballs hard and furious!"

Canadian-born Ian Lee explains the antagonism: "The newcomers were seen the same way as the whites had once looked upon us as kids. Finally acceptance had arrived for us and we felt confident. Then there was this influx of

people who were the same race as us, but who behaved in ways that we didn't want them to behave: they didn't speak the language, they didn't dress the same way, and we said, 'These people are an embarrassment to us!'"

It was not just young Chinese Canadians who looked askance at the newcomers. The old-timers who had sponsored them thought them lazy and

Joe Eng playing pool, 1960.

stories with all our might" because they "attack the integrity and loyalty of Chinese Canadians and those about to become Canadian."[15] Eventually, a full rebuttal by Foon Sien was printed by the paper.

In October of 1955 the same newspaper featured an exposé of illegal immigration on its front page.[16] The article charged that 50 to 85 per cent of recent Chinese immigrants used false papers to enter Canada and that Chinese-Canadian sponsors here paid great sums of money for such papers. Chinatown leaders admitted that abuses of the immigration system did occur, but only because the regulations themselves were unfair. Since only relatives of Chinese-Canadian citizens could enter Canada, desperate applicants would make themselves fit those definitions. The Chinese felt they were still being persecuted, that even after twenty-five years of total exclusion, they were still being made to suffer, even as European immigrants were entering Canada freely. While the charges were not

Chinese refugees arriving in Vancouver, 1965. The women use traditional carrying straps to hold infants to their backs.

irresponsible. Jimmy Lum recalls, "The old-timers always thought of us as rebels. They wanted us to work hard, to make money, to follow their way of life. But the young people wanted to get together, to have some fun, to learn things on their own. Some even broke away from their families and moved into hotels or rooming houses."

There was a huge generation gap between these New Canadians and their parents. The young men had experienced Western-oriented education in Hong Kong and China, they played Western sports, and they even sang popular Western songs. "I thought 'steak' was a Chinese word!" says Victor Lee. The newcomers derided the way the older generation passed its time at the communal houses and association halls, talking about old times and playing mah-jong. There was a difference in attitude towards politics, too. According to Victor Lee, "We were more idealistic than the older generation. When we saw injustice, we spoke out and stood up to it, whereas the older generation from practical experience would not."

Vicious arguments sometimes exploded between fathers and sons. Sister Theresa Fung recalls, "Some of the old-timers had come on false papers earlier on, so when one of them took out citizenship and applied for his family to come over, there would be two different names. Later when there was trouble in the family, the son would say, 'You're not really my father, we have different names!'"

No 57273   G.   R.   Port Health Office,
Hong Kong.

HONG KONG

注 射 證 書

INTERNATIONAL CERTIFICATE OF INOCULATION AGAINST ....

姓名
This is to certify that (Name) *Yue Wong Kan Mee*
年齡   性別
(age: 3 8 sex: F), whose photograph appears below/whose passport number and signature appear below, was on the dates indicated inoculated against

Material			Inoculating Officer	
Date	Origin	Batch No. & Type	Signature	Official Position
30 MAY 1950				ASSISTANT PORT HEALTH OFFICER HONG KONG

Signature of person inoculated ....

N.B.—This certificate is not valid for more than .... months from date of issue.

FEE: 50 Cents $2.00

Inoculation certificate for wife of Chinese Canadian as she prepared to join her husband in Canada.

The Hai Fung Club's music troupe performing in 1963.

inaccurate, they focussed negative attention on Chinese Canadians at a time when proving themselves to be good Canadians was of paramount importance.

Then, early on 24 May 1960, the "largest peacetime operation in RCMP history" simultaneously raided Chinese communities across Canada. The largest probes occurred in Vancouver, where thirty officers searched fourteen offices and residences, seizing large quantities of documents. The police were not pursuing the illegal immigrants but attempting to destroy the worldwide, multimillion-dollar immigration industry operating out of Hong Kong. The RCMP estimated that eleven thousand of the twenty-three thousand Chinese arrivals since 1946 had come on false papers.[17]

In June of 1960 the government started an amnesty program to allow illegal immigrants to come forward and adjust their status without fear of prosecution or deportation. Over a thirteen-year period, twelve thousand

New Energy, New Culture

With the infusion of immigrants in the 1950s, the cultural life of Chinatown took on new dimensions. Two notable organizations provided outlets for the newcomers' energies. One was the Chinese Youth Association (CYA). It was openly supportive of the People's Republic of China at a time when China was considered a "red" threat to world democracy. Community elders feared the young people possessed subversive political ambitions, but the organization was merely a focussed outlet for youthful energy and pride.

Jimmy Lum was a member: "We had a dance troupe and since there weren't enough girls, the guys dressed up as girls! We must have been the first Chinese dance group in Vancouver. We listened to music tapes, watched movies,

Foon Sien chairs a meeting at the Chinese Benevolent Association regarding the city's urban renewal plans to bulldoze Chinese homes in Strathcona, September 1960.

Chinese did so. But the government grew impatient and police raided five Chinatown associations and two residences in Vancouver in July of 1961. Under the banner headline "Terrorists Silence Chinese Immigrants," the minister of justice claimed that immigration brokers were terrorizing their clients to prevent them from helping the police.[18] Nothing came of this charge. By this time, even the Vancouver *Sun* editorialized "Call Off the Hounds" because "all that's being accomplished is to hold Canadian justice up to ridicule."[19]

During this era, Chinese Canadians were invariably associated with illicit entry into Canada. Major Canadian magazines carried lengthy articles on the topic, such as "How Chinese Are Smuggled into Canada: Defeating Our Immigration Laws Is a Lucrative Racket" (*Weekend*, 29 April 1961) and "The Criminal Society that Dominates the Chinese in Canada" (*Maclean's*, 7 April 1962).

In 1962 racial discrimination was

reduced in Canadian immigration policy when skill level was set as the main criterion for entry. In 1967 a point system was introduced that allowed Chinese applicants to be assessed in the same way as other immigrants. Finally, Chinese who were not sponsored by relatives and who qualified on the merit of their own skills were allowed to enter Canada.

Redevelopment Threatens Chinatown

As the battle over immigration slowed in the early 1960s, Chinatowns all across Canada faced destruction under government plans for urban renewal. In 1957 Strathcona was pinpointed as one such area. The three levels of government combined to acquire blocks of houses, bulldoze them, and erect public housing projects. Displaced homeowners could either move into the new housing or they were on their own. The overall plan would eventually displace nine thousand Chinese over a twenty-year period. The threat was clear: removing the adjacent

To celebrate its sixth anniversary, the Yen-ping Youth Association sponsored a basketball tournament in 1964. The teams included Hai Fung, United Labour, Hon Hsing, Britannia Alumni, Freemasons, and Yen-ping.

read books, and then we created dances. We got a few lessons from the girls at the Russian People's Hall. We performed there too, and at the Ukrainian Hall, at labour picnics, and over in Nanaimo.

"There were lots of activities at CYA. We published a newspaper. We had a choir: everyone was a singer in those days. We had drama, we did skits. Every Saturday night there was a gathering: we'd

perform and sing songs, play games and puzzles. It was the only entertainment we had."

The other key new organization was Hai Fung, a literary, sports, and arts club formed in 1957. But it too was viewed suspiciously by the old guard in Chinatown and labelled Communist.

"Individual members may have identified quite strongly with the new China, which is quite natural," recalls member

Recess time at Lord Strathcona School, 1961. In the postwar era, the Strathcona neighbourhood, as well as its school, became predominantly Chinese.

Teenagers gathered around Roger Lowe and his drum set at the Chinese Benevolent Association, 1954.

Tse Shui-yim. ''No matter how innocent you were, you were still accused. All you could do was to start things that were good for the community and let actions speak for themselves. You couldn't go around wearing a badge proclaiming, 'I'm not Communist!''''

There was the very popular basketball tournament series that Hai Fung helped organize in Chinatown. Tse Shui-yim:

''There were at least six to eight Chinese-Canadian teams: Hon Hsing, the Freemasons, Britannia Alumni, and so on at the Gibbs Boys' Club. The tournament was quite something because it was the first one in years! Of course heavy betting among the spectators was involved too. At that time, I was angry about the gambling, but, to think of it now, it was part of the fun!''

Hai Fung also sponsored a ping-pong tournament called the Chinatown Open: ''All the big trophies were won by whites in those first years because we weren't that good yet. And people in Chinatown said, 'Gee you're stupid. You set up everything and then you let the whites take all the big trophies!' Well, we saw things differently. We wanted to expand our scope beyond Chinatown.''

As Chinatown changed in the postwar years, some buildings were renovated, while others, like this residential and commercial building at Hastings and Columbia (southwest corner), were demolished, 1959.

Racism

According to Andrew Joe, in 1947 Vancouver saw ''the beginning of the change from being one of the most racist cities in Canada to one which is now the most democratic. It was a tremendous qualitative change.''

LARRY WONG: *When I graduated from high school in '57, I went down to the bank on Pender Street and asked for a job as a teller. At that time,* the manager said, ''Well, can you speak Chinese?''

I said, ''No I can't, but what's the difference?''

He said, ''I tell you what, I'll send you to the head office.''

So I went and talked to the personnel people there, and they still asked me the same question, ''Can you speak Chinese?''

I said, ''No. I suppose if I did, I would only be working in Chinatown.''

Larry Wong, 1987.

They said, ''Yes.''

I said, ''What's wrong with my working at some other branch elsewhere in the city?''

They said, ''Well, it's because some of our customers may not like dealing with a Chinese person.''

That really threw me off.

DONNA CHAN: *I remember making reservations at a restaurant, and instead of using a very Oriental name like Chan, I would use Lee,*

residential base would kill commercial Chinatown. Some Chinese families saw this as a chance to move up and out, but many others remained deeply attached to the neighbourhood.

Despite protests from Chinese property owners led by Foon Sien, Phase One began in 1960, bulldozing thirty acres to build the MacLean Park highrise and the Raymur-Campbell public housing project. An estimated 860 people, excluding boarders and transients, were displaced, and over half this number were Chinese.[20]

In January of 1963 Foon Sien resigned in protest from the City's Redevelopment Consultative Committee, which had ratified Phase Two. At this point, the mayor invited the Chinese to submit their own plans for a block bounded by Keefer, Jackson, Georgia, and Dunlevy streets, but the two plans that were proposed were rejected. Phase Two went ahead in July of that year, displacing twenty-three hundred people, mostly Chinese.[21] The wholesale uprooting and demolition

continued until 1968, when the Strathcona Property Owners' and Tenants' Association was formed and fought successfully to institute a self-help rehabilitation program.

The people of Chinatown eventually won one of the battles along the way. In June of 1967 city council declared its intention to accept plans for a waterfront freeway linked to the Georgia Viaduct by a Chinatown connector. The connector was an eight-lane, two-hundred-foot-wide, thirty-foot-high freeway cutting east along Carrall. It would eat up three-quarters of the historic block of East Pender.[22] When Chinatown protested, council asked its planners for an alternative route, but there was none.

When council voted to accept the plan that summer, a massive protest erupted from many quarters of the city. Architecture and planning students from the university marched down Pender Street, and black banners were hung from Chinatown balconies.[23] Over a hundred people representing Chinese-

Canadian organizations attended a CBA meeting and nominated a seventeen-member committee to fight the freeway. At public hearings the Community Arts Council, the local chapter of the Architectural Institute, and the Board of Trade all protested city hall's planned freeway. Council eventually rescinded its Carrall Street decision in January of 1968.

By this time, many changes occurred. Public expressions of racism decreased. A brand new component of immigrant people enlarged the community. Chinese Canadians seized opportunities to leave Chinatown and pursue greater white acceptance and assimilation. Many moved out of Chinatown, but business and community activity continued to be focussed there.

---

something that wasn't quite as obvious. There was a feeling that you wouldn't be given as good a table and things like that.

IAN LEE: There was always something. You'd go to a store and either get no service or have to wait an awfully long time for it. In the early fifties, the kids wore strider pants, and if they were made of black denim, they'd call them Chink pants, because they were

usually tailored at a store in Chinatown. Or they'd say, "Let's go down to Chink town and get some Chink food." It was hard to deal with. Or they'd say, "Don't go to a Chinese restaurant, they feed you cat food." And soya sauce they called "horse-blood."

I was going to take up a trade of some kind, but you could not get membership in a trade union if you were Chinese. These were all

unwritten regulations, they just never accepted you. Everybody said that you would be lucky to get a job. Virtually all the Granville Street beer parlours and hotels would not serve Orientals. I don't think the Chinese felt things had changed substantially, other than the fact that we got the vote.

When we were first living together down in the West End, trying to get an

apartment was really quite funny. We would see a house with a "Flat for Lease" sign in the window and we would stop and as soon as we walked up the path, somebody would take the sign out. Then they would tell us that the flat had already been rented. This was 1963.

Vancouver Chinese Girls' Drill Team

The Vancouver Chinese Girls' Drill Team, formed in 1958, was officially sponsored by the Chinese Benevolent Association. It performed precision drills and marching patterns in Western military tradition. The team incorporated baton twirling, drums, and colourful Chinese costumes into its numbers, and was a popular parade feature in Vancouver and other cities until the mid-sixties. Donna Chan was team captain and drill instructor for the team when it started.

A group of us were just sitting and chatting one evening after a get-together and again that feeling came up of, "Here we are at the Pender Y, attending dances with Glen Miller songs and all that. But we're in Chinatown! What's there that's Chinese? We know we're different. But what's there to do to make us proud?"

We knew that Victoria had a drill team and we had seen the Seattle girls come here and perform. Someone said, "Wouldn't it be nice if we had something like that?" And that's where it all started.

We started at home with sugar cube formations to plan our steps and patterns, and then we practised in the Strathcona yard and then at the Ding Ho parking lot. The parents and some of the merchants of Chinatown were really supportive. At the highest point, we had about fifty girls for one of our parades.

They're Happy Together

Urban renewal promised a clean new look for Strathcona. The wooden houses from the turn of the century would be replaced by public housing apartments and row homes. But the concrete would replace more than just houses. It threatened a way of life that had been nurtured for many years. There were family homes and communal houses that bachelor men long separated from the families in China had set up. This account from the 7 January 1961 edition of the Vancouver *Sun* takes the reader into one such house.

A three-storey stucco house at 428 Keefer contains twelve old men, a thousand and one memories and the reason many city Chinese are bucking slum clearance.

For thirty-seven years, men from the small village of Hing Mee in southern China have found sanctuary in this house.

A visit Friday showed twelve contented men, warming themselves around the oil heater in the chair-lined parlor, meditating, writing letters.

Bowls of plants and flowers almost hid a table. A decanter of the best scotch and a battery of shot glasses was brought from under the blooms.

"Happy New Year," said the twelve old men, glasses high.

Narrow strips of red paper covered half the wall. These bore the names of society members, most now subsisting on meagre pensions and planting and harvest wages, who still found money to send to the less fortunate back in Hing Mee village.

Yuletide decorations criss-crossed the ceiling.

Sepia-colored pictures of Dr. Sun Yat-sen and Chiang Kai-shek hung in honour.

In the pungent kitchen with its proud new six-burner gas plate, a tenant sat on a bench at a long table, spooning greens from a bowl of broth.

Doors and stairways to the second and third floors are painted flaming Chinese red. Up here are four bedrooms, shared by the twelve tenants, all bachelors or widowers.

In this house, the members of the Hing Mee Society sleep as late as they want. They eat what they like to eat. They invite their relatives in each spring for a little party. They are happy.

They would like to remain together for the rest of their lives, village boys who grew up together and want to die together.

Slum clearance means they probably will be split up. [26]

Douglas Jung

In the June 1962 federal election, Douglas Jung, Member of Parliament for Vancouver Centre, lost the seat. He had served the riding since 1957 and had represented Canada at the United Nations. Jung blamed his defeat on the police crackdown on illegal Chinese immigration, which had raised considerable ire in Chinatown. "I'm the fall guy," he said. "I was beaten by my own people."

The Vancouver *Sun* featured two editorials on the item: one from *Chinatown News* and one of its own. Excerpts from the *Sun* commentary are below.

Mr. Jung's defeat by little more than five hundred votes was preceded by a bitter campaign in Chinatown. Since he was the first Chinese Canadian to be elected to Parliament, [Chinatown News] *also sees the defeat as a setback for all Chinese Canadians.*

With the last we cannot agree.

Chinese-Canadian pride—a lively and justified sentiment-cannot but be bruised by the ousting of that race's only MP from Parliament. There is little doubt that if all Chinese Canadians in Vancouver Centre had voted, and voted unanimously for Mr. Jung, he would have been re-elected.

That Chinatown did not so vote is a sign of its political maturity.

If Chinese Canadians had voted en masse for Mr. Jung because he was a Chinese Canadian, it would have confirmed the assessment of them as a minority group, set apart from other Canadians. Doubtless the issues on which they split were of special concern to Chinese Canadians, but they split and voted on the issues, not on the race of the candidate.

They voted as adult, independent-thinking individuals, not as a minority group. As Canadians among Canadians. It is to their credit. [27]

The "bachelors" of early Chinatown were still a part of the community in the 1970s. These old-timers were joined in numbers by other seniors, the parents of more recent immigrants.

Saltwater Centennial: Old-timers and Newcomers

By 1986, the year of Saltwater City's centennial, things had changed dramatically. Vancouver's Chinatown had been designated a provincial historic area in 1971, and city hall passed zoning bylaws to protect the area's architecture. Some 150,000 Chinese lived in Greater Vancouver, but the majority were new immigrants. Since 1967 they had arrived in increasing numbers from Hong Kong, China, the South Pacific, Southeast Asia, South America, and Africa. They overwhelmed in number the descendants of the pioneers and the families reunited during the 1950s. More importantly, they raised new issues of visibility for all Chinese Canadians.

The most visible changes occurred on the streets of Chinatown. Armed with a fierce business savvy forged in the highly competitive Asian marketplaces, the immigrants opened new stores that pushed the boundaries of Chinatown farther and farther out. Shops selling fashions, jewellery, music, and fresh foods multiplied, as did *dim-sum* houses, fast-food noodle outlets, and bakery-cafés. The price of land skyrocketed and storefronts all along Pender Street gleamed with a sleek modern look. Several small-scale shopping malls went up as Chinese-speaking doctors, lawyers, stockbrokers, and travel agents serviced immigrants who did not live nearby but who needed to speak in Chinese.

Business was booming, but the Canadian-borns and old-timers were muttering, "It used to be that you could walk down Pender Street and know everybody's name. Nowadays, I walk down Pender Street and I'm the stranger!" Still, they breathed with relief and pride that Pender Street had escaped the urban renewal bulldozers that had destroyed other Chinatowns across Canada. Chinatown reminded them of their unique stake in the past. They knew that they had been here first and complained that the new immigrants didn't appreciate their efforts: "They come to Canada today and they've got rights, they can vote, and the government helps them out. It's a paradise for them! Do you think it was so easy for us? Do you think they'd have such a good time if it weren't for us?"

Sometimes the reception was downright hostile. One 1969 immigrant who worked at a sawmill recalled, "As soon as the old-timers saw us, they didn't like us. We were young, we were strong, so they were jealous of us. But they weren't jealous of the Indians or the whites who came along. Why? The old-timers were afraid that when the white foreman looked at all the Chinese, he would pick the young workers and not the old ones."

The Canadian-borns were fast disappearing into mainstream Canada. Their children had grown up away from Chinatown without learning Chinese. One mother explained, "Just getting the kids through school, concentrating on being good citizens, exploring all their

Wing and Esther Wong ran a store selling candies, patent medicines, comic books, newspapers, cold drinks, and toys for many years at Gore and Pender, c. 1975.

talents or no talents, and trying different things was a lot of work. Learning Chinese wasn't that important. What was important was relating to everyone and feeling comfortable with yourself. It didn't matter that you had black hair."

After decades of discrimination, racist attitudes had changed to open up career doors and social opportunities. The third and fourth generations could now cut ties with Chinatown. But at this key juncture, at the very time it was most possible to become invisible, the massive arrival of newcomers pulled Chinese Canadians back into a community of immigrants, at least in the eyes of white society and in the politics of Chinatown.

Hong Kong Money

The new immigrants were a different breed. They were not as desperate or as disadvantaged as the pioneer arrivals. The greatest number of newcomers came from Hong Kong, the British Crown Colony exporting rich and working-class emigrants. The well-

Romy So and her family with well-wishers at Hong Kong airport just prior to departing for Vancouver, 1969.

Becoming Canadian

The new immigrants of recent years came with skills. They also came at different ages and were transformed into Canadians in many ways.

Romy So's family came in 1969 when she was thirteen, and she recalls how hard it was for her father. He had been a bookkeeper in Macao, but here he worked as a labourer in a Chinatown market. "It was heavy work, and he had a

rough time. His coworkers spoke Toisan and didn't understand his Cantonese. So my father always wanted to go back. Then he lost his eyesight. He was amazed at Canada's welfare system because he knew we wouldn't have survived back in Macao."

The teenage years are difficult in any culture. Many teens from Hong Kong did not think they would stay here but would return to Hong Kong or

Tommy Tao shortly after arriving in Canada. One of the new challenges was the Canadian winter.

China. They proudly considered themselves a different breed from the Chinese in China and Taiwan because their cultural roots had been taken from China and planted in British colonial soil.

After teenager Tommy Tao arrived in 1968, he wrote frequently to his friends in Hong Kong. They discussed China, Chinese politics, and Chinese literature. Then he discovered he had changed:

to-do possessed professional or technical skills and a working knowledge of English. They had put their children in English schools in Hong Kong, had attended Western symphony concerts and modern art shows, and had inherited Hong Kong's dynamic fusion of old and modern forms of Chinese expression. Adapting to Canada was relatively easy for these immigrants, who were confident and conversant with both Chinese and Western cultural forms.

They were also being lured into Canada. Since the mid-1970s, a federal government hungry for business capital had been encouraging entrepreneurs to enter Canada. Applicants who could bring in $250,000 and start a business creating at least one new Canadian job could immigrate readily. In the first half of 1983 Hong Kong entrepreneurs brought into Canada $300 million, half of which came to British Columbia.[1]

Hong Kong money, of course, had been entering Vancouver since 1967, when the push to emigrate suddenly accelerated. That year, China's Cultural Revolution swept into Hong Kong. For several months there were strikes, demonstrations, bombings, and martial law. It was an uneasy reminder that 1997, the year Hong Kong would revert to ownership by China, was approaching. Businessmen fearful of living under a Communist government began to make plans to move their money and families abroad.

Early reaction to Hong Kong money was negative. One Vancouver alderman's 1973 comments resembled racist accusations used against an earlier generation of Chinese. He said, "They've built all the cheap buildings they could in Hong Kong and now they're moving in here. They are driving up the cost of real estate. They are not coming here to be part of the community. They are coming here purely and simply for speculative gain." But local real estate experts refuted these statements immediately.[2]

By the mid-1980s Hong Kong money was seen as a much-needed boon

At the Tak Kee Restaurant, 1975. Many of the restaurants and stores opened by new immigrants were family operations. Some were fancy and expensive, others were not.

"It was during the Canada-Russia hockey series in 1972. I remember watching the Canadians being soundly beaten in the first few games and then battling back to snatch victory from the jaws of defeat. By the final game, Bobby Clark, Paul Henderson, and Ken Dryden had become my heroes. I was cheering for Team Canada and getting very emotional about the whole thing!"

Immigrant teenagers also had to deal with parents who were set in their ways. Romy So knew she had changed, but her parents had not.

"I couldn't tell them about school because they would never understand. They never accepted what I said. They always told me right away what was right or wrong, like dating, going out, dances. They always pulled out this old Chinese proverb: 'Work makes strength, play makes waste.' So if there was a field trip or something, I had to lie or withold information. Then I'd feel guilty. You wanted to make your parents happy, but how could you do it if you were miserable?"

Becoming Canadian is a subtle process, but after undergoing some change, an immigrant's perspective is different. "I hear my immigrant friends and relatives criticizing the Canadian-borns for not speaking Chinese or not appreciating the Chinese way of life," sighs Tommy Tao. "Yet it's ironic, because those people will have Canadian-born kids or grandchildren themselves!"

Others see themselves as bridges between two cultures. Wendy Jang came at age eight in 1965, and her younger brothers and sisters are Canadian-born. "My parents

Restaurant work: dim-sum chef, 1975.

are very Chinese—they still pray to the ancestors on special days. My brothers and sisters just laugh. But I understand these things because I went through all that in Hong Kong."

The option of going back has changed, too. "I've gone back to Hong Kong twice since coming to Canada," a thoughtful Sandra Wilking says. "And each trip has reaffirmed my desire to stay

here and to be a Canadian. After being a foreign student, now an immigrant, now a citizen, the whole experience has made me more curious, curious about Canada, curious about Canadians. And the knowledge gained from that has made me very obligated, in the sense of wanting to contribute to this country in whatever way I can. I want to do my part in building this nation."

From Around the World

Recent Chinese immigrants have come to Vancouver from around the world. What do they bring with them? Some come with very little. Bank manager Bill Ma left Calcutta, India, in 1964: "I was a businessman and our company had some four hundred employees, but that didn't mean anything because of the political unrest. When we came over here we had no

friends, no relatives, and no money. My family of five was allowed to bring twenty-four dollars and myself eight dollars."

Others, like Nelly Law from Lima, Peru, came with images of Vancouver they had seen in magazines. "The gorgeous surroundings, the big mountains with a bit of snow on top, the huge streets, and the cleanness of the city made such a big impression on me."

Not all Chinese came to Vancouver directly. Charlie San left Laos and lived in Quebec for seven years. Because there were so few Asians there, he remembers Quebeckers being very friendly to him. Sandra Wilking came to Vancouver from South Africa, via Hong Kong. Having learned French in high school, she thought she'd use it here in Canada. "What a rude shock to find out you had to use English," she recalls.

As strangers in a strange land, the newcomers proved keen to learn. "When I came to university," Sandra Wilking continues, "I was eager to get to know Canadians because I believe if you come to a new country, you've got to try and understand it. What I found was that Canadian Caucasians didn't know much about Chinese people. I got asked a lot about Chinese food and about which restaurant to go to. It puzzled me at first, and then I understood. It was their lack of contact."

Others who came from Hong Kong were disappointed. Wendy Jang came at age eight in 1965 and heard people in Hong Kong calling Canada "Gold Mountain." "So I thought it was going to have big mansions and modern houses. Well, I came and when I saw the old airport, it was a big shock. Coming to Canada was nothing like the dreams I had."

Homesickness hit all new immigrants, but Nelly Law says, "We thought as immigrant Canadians we had to work twice as hard. I think we still have to do that in order to prove ourselves."

One adjustment problem was food. Sandra Wilking recalls going into a Chinatown restaurant shortly after arriving. "I was just devastated. The food was not very good. I thought, my goodness, how am I going to survive?"

A more serious issue is language. Julie Chen came from Guangzhou, China, in 1981. "Sometimes people look down at me because I'll say something wrong. They make fun of me and make me ashamed. And I can't fight with them because they know more English. So I just walk away."

Of course, there were basic cultural differences too. Teacher Mimie Ho came over in 1967 and taught in Clearwater, British Columbia, for a year. "When the kids said 'moose,' I didn't know what they were talking about. And teachers are treated so differently here. In Hong Kong, the kids bow to say 'good morning,' and everyone respects the teacher. Even when the teacher is wrong, they'll say the teacher is right. In Hong Kong, you can punish the students, but here you have to be so encouraging."[7]

Store clerk unloading wooden crates, c. 1975. The businesses of Chinatown continued to provide jobs for many Chinese, especially those who did not speak English fluently.

Jack Say Yee, c. 1975.

Names in the News: Politicians

When visible minorities are elected to office, there is good reason to celebrate. It means that the larger society has nodded approval and placed its trust in one of "us." Vancouver has elected Chinese Canadians to all three levels of government.

Jack Say Yee

A psychiatric social worker and clinical counsellor, Vancouver-born Jack Say Yee became the first Chinese Canadian elected to the school board in 1973. He had attended Strathcona Elementary: "I grew up in the slums. My dad ran the Butler Hotel at 110 Water Street. My playmates were drunks, prostitutes, down-and-outers, veterans who had come back from the war as social misfits. Everybody said, 'Poor Jack, he's from the slums.' That

The gala opening of the Chinese Cultural
Centre in 1980.

144

to the Canadian economy. In a cover
story entitled "The Richest Refugees:
How Hong Kong Capitalism Is
Reshaping Our Economy," the May
1987 issue of *Canadian Business*
magazine profiled several entrepreneurs
and showed how they were energizing
Canadian business and broadening
Canada's commercial horizons. The
article concluded, "Chinese
immigration has been a permanent
feature of Canadian society for more
than a century. Now they're coming
again, and Canada needs them as much
now as we did a century ago—this time
to help revitalize our economy."

When Hong Kong people arrived in
Vancouver, they bolstered its Chinese
presence. Their sophisticated taste buds
boosted standards of Chinese food.
They opened acclaimed restaurants
throughout the city and created a new
Chinatown in Richmond in 1987. They
donated significant sums to build the
Chinese Cultural Centre and the Dr.
Sun Yat-sen Classical Garden, two
ambitious, multimillion-dollar projects.

made me even more deter-
mined."[8]
Art Lee
Art Lee grew up in Alberta,
where the only discrimination
he experienced took place
when white kids mistook him
for a Native Indian. When he
came to Vancouver, he spoke
Toisanese but not Cantonese.
He laughs, "It made great
newspaper copy to show me in
a language lab taking Chinese
lessons!"

Lee was elected to
Parliament in 1974 as a Liberal
and got involved immediately
with the Green Paper on
Immigration. For the first time
he became conscious of being
perceived as a Chinese person,
as opposed to a Canadian of
Chinese descent. "In the
Green Paper there was a badly
written reference to 'Canadians
of novel and distinctive
features.' So I got up at the
hearings and said, 'Hey, I'm

Election brochure for Art Lee.

one of those guys with the
novel and distinctive
features.'"

On the head tax question: "I
knew how much head tax had
been collected, so every time I
went for money for a housing
project or a grant, I'd tease my
colleagues by saying, 'You can
take this off our head tax
account.'"
Bill Yee
Lawyer Bill Yee also came
from Chinatown. He started

work as a bus boy at the Bamboo Terrace at age fifteen, two years after his arrival in 1959 without any knowledge of English. Since then, he has sat on many boards, including those of the Chinese Cultural Centre, the Chinese Benevolent Association, and SUCCESS, before becoming the first Chinese-Canadian alderman in Vancouver in 1982.

"My father, his partners, and all the old-timers had one hell of a time. They had to pay the head tax, they could only get low-paying jobs, they had no chance to learn English, they were separated from their families, and they had to work their butts off. I felt I was more fortunate because I was educated."

New Models

Politicians are often assumed to represent their ethnic group. Although they never deny their roots, neither do they want to appear to be lobbying exclusively for that group's interests. Bill Yee commented:

"When I was on city council, I wanted to show that visible minorities could do a good job in the political process. They were not in it just to look after their own kind. But I also wanted to show visible minorities that they should get involved, to vote, to stand up for their rights, to show politicians that they had to be reckoned with.

"I see Canada as a model for our future world. As populations grow, as boundaries are eliminated, we'll have to live together as mankind, not as people from different cultures and countries. We'll have to learn to share, to live peacefully and constructively with each other. I want to generate more acceptance and enthusiasm for that model."

The 1975 Autumn Festival saw the first-ever grass dragon in Vancouver's Chinatown. Following traditional plans, grass was cut from Fraser Valley fields, then coiled into a long snake, from which incense sticks spiked out.

They supported the annual Chinese New Year parade in Chinatown, which attracted thousands of Vancouverites. Chinese pay-TV started in 1983, and new cultural organizations included the Penjing (Chinese bonsai) Society and the Western Canada Chinese Martial Arts Association, which competed in the annual international tournament in China.

The Boat People

But there were also negative spin-offs that worried Chinese Canadians. The on-going public issue of immigration, with citizens asking what kinds of people Canada should take in, was a disturbing reminder that not all Canadians saw this as a multicultural country.

The Vietnam War pushed another, different kind of Chinese into Vancouver. From Saigon's surrender in May 1975 to December 1978, Canada accepted nine thousand refugees from Vietnam. Then, in late 1978, news headlines exploded with the desperate

Racism: How Should We React?

In the spring of 1978 the University of British Columbia campus newspaper was deluged with letters from Chinese-Canadian students. A "humorous" racist article had appeared in a residence newsletter, and the administration had censored subsequent issues. The newsletter editor claimed Asian students had previewed the article and had not found it offensive. But after the issue came out, others did.[9]

One Chinese-Canadian student complained stridently: "Attempts at racist humor such as that in *The Pole* article serve to feed subconscious racism. The more it grows, the more difficult it is to reject and the more acceptable it becomes.

"A brother said to me last night, 'Sure, I read the article. I didn't like it but I don't object.' Dammit! We should object. Every time we turn the other cheek like that, people start to feel that they have a licence to slap our cheeks. Every time we accommodate racism we make it grow. It carries all of us, white, Chinese, or whatever, backward."

Another Chinese-Canadian student challenged him: "A student at a liberal arts university should not be so apt to absorb insults. Rather, one should be more apt to allow offensive gestures to pass as outlets of tension. By rallying against racism, you will only exacerbate more prejudice. Try to integrate with the rest of us and not to consolidate with your 'brothers and sisters.' If you consolidate, then your ethnic group will be seen as another undesirable force."

Their opinions showed how wide a gulf assimilation had

tales of refugee boat people and rape and piracy on the open seas. Canada took in another fifty thousand refugees, most of whom were ethnic Chinese. In Vancouver, Chinese social service organizations such as SUCCESS, the Chinese Benevolent Association, and the Chinese Cultural Centre formed the Vietnamese Refugees Assistance Association in August of 1978 to sponsor and help resettle refugees.

The refugee crisis brought out the best and worst in Canadians across the country. Church groups and private organizations sponsored refugee families and helped them resettle. Many citizens recalled their own immigrant and refugee roots and urged that more help be extended. On the other hand, letters like these appeared in the Vancouver *Sun*:

There are already 100,000 Chinese living in the Greater Vancouver area. Taking into account how rapidly those people multiply, it won't be long before they'll outnumber us two to one.
(25 July 1979)

A community centre was built by the Parks Board in Strathcona in 1972. It served the entire neighbourhood and also offered many programs for the increasing number of seniors in the area.

Washroom wall, Main Library, University of British Columbia, 1987.

created. Writer One wrote a rebuttal: "Ethnic jokes and slurs hurt all people by making them less sensitive to one another. They hurt us too unless we are completely lacking in pride as Chinese people. You seem to suggest that this pain is all in our minds, that if we could just desensitize our minds enough, it wouldn't hurt."

Writer Two then revealed that he knew racism existed more broadly but felt pessimistic about changing things. "What do you do with these people? Beat them up in hopes of them liking you better and respecting your ancestry? Perhaps you will want to get other people who were discriminated against and rally, thus segregating and calling attention to yourselves (a prime target for abuse). This may work against governments, but not racists."

Strathcona Chinese Dance Company performing, 1987.

his work ranges from teaching teachers about human rights legislation to teaching kids about ethnic cooking. He says, ''Really, multiculturalism isn't about content. Kids don't have to learn what the Chinese New Year is. But they do need to acquire an attitude towards fairness and equity. We want them to behave in a fair and just manner towards all people, no matter what they look like, even if it's someone who's spiked his purple hair.''

The cultural forms brought from abroad are seen to enrich the fabric of Canadian life. Some forms are more accessible than others. Raymond Leung taught Chinese martial arts at Vancouver's universities and has seen things change: ''Chinese culture has two complementary parts: the scholarly and the martial. It's easier to teach the martial arts because it involves body and movement. It used to be that the Chinese instructors wouldn't teach Westerners,

but it's wrong to think that if we teach them, they'll use it to beat us. With every new student, I think we make one new friend.''

The cultural forms also change when they arrive. Mimie Ho founded the Strathcona Chinese Dance Company in 1972. ''A lot of traditional Chinese dance is really slow. Westerners like dances that are up-tempo, they like variety, they like to see colour. One of our most requested pieces is Joyful Festival, a medley of popular dances with ribbons and fans and the northern lions.''

Ultimately, culture is related to identity. Immigrants seek out forms familiar and meaningful to them. University of British Columbia librarian Yim Tse, for example, turned to calligraphy to deal with news of his mother's death. Later, he organized calligraphy exhibitions. But accessibility has cropped up as a problem: he has seen people frightened

Other letters were sarcastic and angry with Writer Two's ''banana attitude'' (yellow outside, white inside). One writer summarized them all: ''What I was trying to say, and trying very hard to say was, 'Look, human beings, you've hurt another human being who is made out of the same flesh and blood that you are made of.' If we want to live in harmony with each other, we can only do so when we accept each other on equal terms.''

Rethinking Culture

Multiculturalism is a key word that crops up frequently in discussions of government funding, race relations, school policy, and the arts. People usually think of culture as a luxury, as entertainment to turn to after the rent is paid and the children are safe in bed. But multiculturalism is more than just visiting festivals to watch dancers in exotic costumes and taste foreign foods. There are two aspects of it: race relations and heritage preservation.

Eric Wong is the race relations consultant for the Vancouver School Board, and

Eric Wong, race relations consultant, 1987.

Street activities during a Chinese Cultural Centre festival, c. 1975.

off because they cannot read the Chinese characters.

"Reading the characters is not as important as seeing how they are expressed," Tse explains. "People should approach calligraphy the same way they approach painting, seeing it as an abstract form of expression. Look how the brush does wonders with variations. The tones can be dry or wet, the size of characters small or large."

Mimie Ho sees Chinese dance as a recreational activity for children. "I don't pretend to be a dance school. I hope the children learn something about their own identity and culture through dance. It builds up their self-confidence and personality. The kids love to do it: they're ready to give up other things to stay in the group."

And what about those who choose not to participate in cultural forms associated with the Old Country? Artists such as painter Raymond Chow, composer Alexina Louie, and potter Wayne Ngan are successful in their own right. They are part of mainstream culture, not multicultural culture. Perhaps one day there will not be such a separation.

In the late 1960s Vancouver-born Raymond Chow gained a reputation for capturing on paper the older buildings of Vancouver soon to disappear under the bulldozer. He exhibited all across Canada and in San Francisco and in London, England.

Interracial Marriages

Interracial marriages are a common, accepted fact of life in Vancouver today. Such marriages often start out under a cloud of disapproval and worry that soon clears up, especially after a grandchild is born. In many cases, the relationship started out innocently and unexpectedly. "Ever since I was little, I thought I'd marry someone Chinese," confesses Selina Chew, a second-generation Canadian. "That was part of growing up. I never thought it could be otherwise. I didn't go around looking for someone white. When John came

along, he just happened to be white."

Dating was the first step, and parental response was predictable. Susan Kong, who is a third-generation Canadian, had dated white men. "When they came to the house, my dad would be really rude, slamming the doors and things like that." She was baffled because they had neighbours who were foster parents to Native Indian children. "My dad always talked about how great the people next door were, how they didn't differentiate between white or brown or black."

The next step was telling the family. Selina Chew recalls, "When I told my parents about John, I described him in the most Chinese way possible. I said, 'He has dark hair, and he's not too tall.'"

When Susan Kong told her father she was moving out to live with David, "He blew up. He didn't have to say anything. Chinese fathers just give you that incredible look of disapproval. I knew I wouldn't be considered his daughter for a while. But my mother was always supportive."

Selina Chew's parents were similarly displeased about her marriage plans. "More than anything, they were worried about what their friends and relatives would say. It was a sign of disgrace for them. Remember, I come from a really traditional family: my mother didn't come over until 1954. They could either disown me or put up with John. They decided to do the latter."

Sometimes the marriage was the turning point when parents changed heart. Susan Kong went home the night before the wedding. "When I got dressed, my dad finally talked to me and said that I

Informal kinds of business, such as this egg vendor, were familiar sights on the streets of Chinatown, 1972.

SALTWATER CENTENNIAL

· · · · ·
151

They are Chinese, and as such should go to China. All this money being spent on them should go to our own poor, sick, destitute and old people. I still think most of this is a racket anyway. They look remarkably healthy and well fed to me.
(31 July 1979)

Youth Gangs

The other negative issue linked to the newcomers related to crime. In 1973 the Vancouver Police Department initiated a patrol in Chinatown to investigate an increase in unreported crimes and the start of youth gangs. In one instance a gang had demanded free admission to a Chinese movie house. When the manager tried to phone the police, his office was invaded and he was warned not to touch the phone if he ever wanted to walk in Chinatown again. The doorman let the gang in.

School Trustee Jack Say Yee cited unrealistic expectations as one cause of the problem. "Traditionally, Chinese parents want their children to achieve at the highest level, and this usually means university. They put pressure on the children and they can't cope because of the language difficulty. The children are trying to live in two worlds: conform to the old ways at home and be Canadian in school."[3]

This situation usually confronted the unskilled and semiskilled immigrant families. Many had come from the crowded resettlement estates of Hong Kong. Others from rural, socialist China or Vietnam were even less educated and less equipped to learn English and find jobs. But the higher cost of living forced both parents to work, often at low wages and for long hours, which cut them off from their children. Social worker Jonathan Lau worked with such families in the early 1970s and observed the following:

Their parents are working hard, and there tends to be a lack of family discipline, family management, and a lack of communication in the home. The kids speak English in school but at recess they gather together and revert to

Lawrence Chen, a long-time artisan of Chinatown, painted many of the gold-leaf-on-glass signs in Chinatown, c. 1974.

Jack and Nancy Scott Wong, 1987.

looked really pretty. And at the wedding, my dad was relaxed and smiling. He saw how happy we were and how David came from a good family."

Selina Chew's husband John did not do anything special to win his in-laws over. "No matter what race you are," she says pragmatically, "you'll try to impress your in-laws. My dad spoke broken English, so they had a drink over dinner and that helped

make things okay. And my dad knew that John loved barbecued duck, so every Sunday he brought one home from Chinatown when we came over for dinner."

As for things on the other side? David recalls, "When I told my dad, he said, 'Babies from mixed marriages are really beautiful.' He seemed quite pleased."

Selina Chew: "Acceptance works both ways. When John

told his parents, his dad's first reaction was, 'You're marrying a Chinaman?' John and his mother were astonished at him! So the first time I met him, I was quite cold, because I knew about this statement. Then they found out that I was quite normal, and that the only difference was that I'm Asian."

Some stories were happy from the outset. Nancy Scott Wong tells this tale: "Jack's mother and grandmother had

China Month poster, 1979. A showing of films from China. After normalization of diplomatic relations with China, there was an upsurge of interest in things Chinese.

China Month:
CHINESE FILM FESTIVAL

12 films to be exhibited including New Year Sacrifice, Lin's Family Shop, Fifteen Strings of Cash, Dr. Norman Bethune in China, Liang Shan Bo and Zhu Ying Tai, Serfs, Zhang Ga the Soldier Boy, Women Basketball Players No. 5, The Marriage of a Fairy Princess, Family, Red Guards of Hong Hu and The Magic Lotus Lantern.

A presentation of Pacific Cinematheque
At the National Film Board Theatre, 1155 W Georgia
Members $1.50   Non-Members $2.00
November 14-18 & 21-25, 1979, 7:00, 9:15 & 11:00 p.m.
(Sunday, 1:30 & 3:30 p.m.)

中國月

中國電影節

The Chinese Cultural Centre

In 1978 the proposed Chinese Cultural Centre became the focal point for the last battle of the Cold War and of China's civil war to be fought in Vancouver.

When China and Canada established diplomatic ties in 1970, Taiwan (ruled by the Kuomintang) lost its voice in Canada. Kuomintang supporters then seized control of Vancouver's Chinese Benevolent Association (CBA). In 1967 the CBA had helped buy a full-page ad in *The New York Times* opposing China's entry into the United Nations. The CBA actively supported Taiwan and continually raised the spectre of Communist agents prowling about. The CBA flew the Kuomintang flag and celebrated Taiwan's holidays. No open elections to the CBA board were held, yet it claimed to speak for the local Chinese community.

But the urban renewal protests of the 1970s had created new leaders. In 1972 they joined with a majority of Chinatown's organizations to start planning the Chinese Cultural Centre (CCC), a $6.7 million multiuse complex. This new project fired the energy of all kinds of Chinese Canadians, and hundreds volunteered their time. The CCC's public profile grew quickly as it lobbied governments and rallied community support. It launched festivals, soccer tournaments, legal aid and tax services, and English and citizenship classes, and it sided with the barbecue meat merchants against health officials. Dismayed at the upstart CCC, the CBA backed a new, rival group called the Chinese Canadian Activity Centre (CCAC). The CCAC put forth plans for another cultural centre to stop government funding from reaching the CCC. To discredit the CCC, innuendoes were made that it was infiltrated by Communists. The CBA hoped to capitalize on the vestiges of mistrust held by old-timers who had lost assets in China during land reform. They hoped to play up on the Cold War hysteria to give freedom-loving North Americans no choice but to oppose the Communists. In fact, the CCC's board of bank managers, lawyers, and merchants hardly were leftists.

In 1977 it became evident that the CBA was going to sell its Chinatown building, originally built in 1906 from community donations, to help finance the CCAC. At this point an *ad hoc* coalition of concerned citizens decided to expose the fact that the CBA was foreign-controlled. Both city newspapers carried headlines like "Taiwan Said Plotting Chinatown Takeover" and reported that Taiwan had sent agents and money into Canada.

The coalition sued the CBA for failing to hold regular elections, and the Supreme Court of British Columbia ordered open elections under court supervision. A furious campaign of leafleting ensued. Five thousand people voted in the single largest turnout in the history of a Chinese organization. The reformers won handily, and fund raising for the CCC followed smoothly.

After the dust settled, it was

given up hope that he would ever marry, so they were really relieved when I came along. They thought it was great that I'd marry him. They were thinking, 'What Chinese girl will take him? He's over thirty, greying, and not a doctor or dentist or lawyer!'"

Another encouraging story comes from Ramona Mar: "My mother always said, 'If and when you marry, all I ask is that you marry a good man.' She never said that he had to be Chinese. She even said once, 'You might marry a Chinese, and he may turn out to be a bad man.' There were three girls in our family, so my mother knew it was more important that we find a career and look after ourselves."

"Pender Guy" was an English-language Chinese-Canadian radio program that tried to explore new avenues of cultural and political involvement for Chinese-Canadians who speak English. Its members (c. 1978) included both immigrants and Canadian-borns.

Book booth at Autumn Festival, 1975. The Chinese Cultural Centre's festivals encouraged the involvement of Canadian-born youth who were inspired by Asian-American projects underway in San Francisco. There, a well-articulated political and cultural philosophy about the status of Asians in North American society had emerged from the civil rights, antiwar, and Third World movements.

clear that the two-China issue was finished in Canada. The Cold War red-baiting of the 1950s was irrelevant and a new attitude towards China was emerging. People could enjoy the culture and heritage of China without being branded Commies. The Chinese Cultural Centre at 50 East Pender, completed in 1980, stands as a reminder of this new era. Here, art exhibitions, Chinese- and English-language

Bill Yee (*left*) with other representatives from the Chinese Benevolent Association at Ching Ming observances at Mountain View Cemetery, 1987. Each spring, Chinese families and organizations visit cemeteries to pay their respects to the generations that have gone ahead.

Chinese. From this communication gap, plus a feeling they're being looked down on by both the rich and better educated new arrivals and by the locally born youngsters, frustrations build up and they tend to stick together.[4]

Police concern was spurred by alarming reports from San Francisco's Chinatown of gang warfare and gun battles over gambling and extortion there in the late 1970s. In 1980 Vancouver police estimated two hundred individuals were involved with the gangs. A police report that same year accused Chinese-Canadian criminals and youth gangs of involvement in organized crime involving gambling, prostitution, drugs, and extortion. In the summer of 1984 the Chinatown Merchants Association threatened to hire private security forces to halt a rash of break-ins. The merchants complained there was not enough police presence in Chinatown, but the police chief replied he could not afford extra officers.

Continuing media coverage of this issue dismayed Chinese-Canadian leaders. They feared the community's reputation was being tarnished and the spectre of crime and violence might invite a racist backlash. "Pender Guy," a Chinese-Canadian radio program broadcast in English on CFRO radio, cautioned in 1980 against jumping to conclusions about youth gangs. One of its documentaries featured a criminologist who commented: "Are ten kids standing on a street corner a gang? Are kids that go bowling or go to a show together a gang? Or are kids that steal together a gang? How much and what type of activity must they engage in before they're considered a gang?"

No solutions seemed forthcoming. The police chief stated in 1987 that hiring more Chinese-Canadian police officers would not curb Asian crime. Instead, he suggested that Chinese Canadians should become more willing to report crimes and testify in court to obtain convictions. But Chinatown leaders argued, "We aren't going to get anywhere if the community blames the

---

instruction, and a variety of classes (for example, painting, tai-chi, and choir) are held. There is a multipurpose hall for special events and each year the centre sponsors the Dragon Boat Races as well as a Chinese New Year festival.[10]

Back to Chinatown

Parents of Canadian-born Chinese taught three lessons to their children: "Study hard, be proud, and learn some Chinese!" Of these, learning Chinese was usually the hardest. But these parents did not urge their offspring to get involved in the Chinese community, so consequently few of them did. The parents believed that success was ultimately judged by one's

accomplishments in the mainstream world, and time and effort would be better invested there. Yet, some second-, third-, and fourth-generation Canadian-borns have come back to participate in the community.

Freelance broadcaster Ramona Mar recalls a typical childhood in Burnaby: "When I was growing up, I didn't know anything about being Chinese. I didn't have any

image of myself as Chinese. I never went to Chinatown except for dim-sum, and I didn't speak the language."

Eric Wong admits that he did not develop strong friendships with foreign-born Chinese Canadians until grade six. "There were some deep reasons why I hadn't made friends with this kind of Chinese person before, and it had to do with assimilation. Of course, the symbol of nonas-

police and the police blame the community."

Former alderman Bill Yee agreed that bilingual officers would not solve the situation because youth gangs were rooted in complicated social, cultural, and economic circumstances. Social workers observed that immigrants needed at least three years of English classes to enter vocational school, but they were often pushed out of high school after just a year or two. Half the Vietnamese teens in Vancouver had left behind parents, and Vietnamese boys outnumbered girls seven-to-one because of the dangerousness of escape from their homeland. Yee suggested that only a co-ordinated program of government funding for language training and youth job creation, together with sensitive policing and citizen co-operation, would prevent gangs from growing.

Race Relations Improve

Racism and Chinatown no longer touched every Chinese Canadian, as many did not identify with a

The Autumn Festivals sponsored by the Chinese Cultural Centre in the late 1970s raised funds through the sale of vegetables donated by Chinese farmers.

similation was Chinese school, which I did not attend."

There were many roads leading back to Chinatown. Ramona Mar was taking journalism at the British Columbia Institute of Technology and did some reporting for *Chinatown News*. "I went to cover a protest meeting at the CBA and I met the people from the "Pender Guy" Chinese-Canadian radio program there. I was really bowled over that young Chinese Canadians were doing things relevant to me, like history, issues, and Asian-American music. And I was impressed that they had a perspective."

At about the same time, she encountered racism directly. She went to a downtown disco and discovered that Asians were paying higher cover charges at the door for not drinking enough. "That incident really politicized me. I was furious. I had always thought of myself as Canadian and to be treated differently shook me up."

"Pender Guy" came at the right time for her. It was an English-language radio program that had grown out of a series of Chinese-Canadian youth conferences. Don Yee described their perspective: "We felt that young Chinese, especially Canadian-borns, were too smug. They didn't care about racism, or they shrugged it off as something that happened years ago. We wanted to confront Chinese Canadians and challenge them to look at themselves. Chinese Canadians have a history and in it lies the context of our belonging here in Canada. 'Pender Guy' was to help document the heroes, stories, events, and memories of this culture."

Chinese barbecued meat shop, 1972.
Consumer demand made this a
multimillion-dollar industry in Chinatown.

. . . . .
156

A contingent of Chinese Canadians
marched with their own banners in
Vancouver's annual Peace March, 1986.

Chinese community nor suffer serious
ill-effects because of their Chinese
descent. But energy was summoned
many times to protest unfair treatment.

In 1972 city hall reneged on
housing promises made to Chinese-
Canadian residents in Strathcona. It had
originally assembled land near
Chinatown for urban renewal but sold a
block in 1968 to a private developer to
build housing. It was never built and the
city tried to re-expropriate the land for a
fire-hall. The protest brochure
denounced it as "The Greatest Hoax,
Giveaway, and Rip-off Ever Told: A
Tragedy in Three Parts." An *ad hoc*
committee rallied five hundred people
who marched through Chinatown to the
site. The fire-hall plans were dropped
shortly thereafter, and a housing co-
operative was erected instead.

In June 1973 Chinatown groups
fought city plans to widen a local street
that would have sent heavy truck traffic
through Chinatown and prevent future
development of its western edge where a
cultural centre was planned. The protest

leaflets cried out, "\$2.2 Million for
Freeway to Nowhere!" The plan was
dropped, and the community's energy
turned to building the Chinese Cultural
Centre, which opened in 1980.

There were also skirmishes in the
recurring war between health officials
and Chinese barbecue meat merchants.
City inspectors ordered the meats stored
either below 4.4 degrees or above 60
degrees Celsius to prevent bacterial
growth. But the merchants argued that
such storage ruined the meats' flavour.
"If people got sick eating our
products," said the president of the
Chinatown Barbecue Merchants
Association, "they would have arrested
us long ago."

Twelve merchants stopped selling
the meat, started a petition, and hired a
lawyer to fight the regulations. A
temporary compromise was reached in
July 1973 when the city yielded on
storage temperatures and the
storekeepers agreed to handle the meats
more quickly. In 1978 Vancouver
merchants launched a cross-country

Ramona Mar subsequently
worked with "Pender Guy," the
Fight W5 Committee that
protested a racist television
program, the Committee to
Celebrate the 125th
Anniversary, the Chinese-
Canadian Human Rights
Group, Asian-Canadian
Theatre, and the Chinese
Cultural Centre's *Saltwater
City* exhibition committee.

Eric Wong, the race relations
consultant for the Vancouver

School Board, went through a
reawakening of interest in
Asian culture at university. "I
took all Asian Studies courses.
What I got was a political
education, studying Vietnam,
colonialism, imperialism, and
the Third World."

The politically conscious
Canadian-borns saw that too
narrow a range of images of
Chinese Canadians existed. On
one hand, they were seen as
new immigrants. On the other

Jazz singer Shannon Gunn and her band
regularly performed on Vancouver's jazz
circuit and were featured at the 1987 Asia
Pacific Festival as well as that year's Jazz
Festival.

hand, "There are lots of Chinese in the technical professions today: doctors, dentists, lawyers, pharmacists," Eric Wong continued. "But we don't have enough people in the arts or humanities. I'd like to bring [jazz singer] Shannon Gunn, [photographer] Chick Rice and [video artist] Paul Wong to my classes. I never knew that Ramona Mar was Chinese. I heard her on the radio, and when I found out that she was Chinese, I was elated! It was the opposite reaction to finding out that [rock band] Wang Chung was *not* Chinese!"

The history that older Canadian-borns have lived through has brought them back to Chinatown, too. Dr. Wallace Chung, born in Victoria and chairman of surgery at University of British Columbia Hospital, was chairman of the Chinese Cultural Centre from 1975 to 1987. He notes that Chinese Canadians got the vote just forty years ago. "But things can still be altered. When the Korean War was on, China could have been at war with the U.S. With a stroke of the pen, the War Measures Act could have been enacted and we could have been shipped off like the Japanese. If young people and new immigrants could realize that what we have today wasn't handed to us on a silver platter, then they'll value things more, they'll be motivated to work harder, to do more for the community."

Art exhibit poster, 1981. Paintings sent over from China for exhibition and sale in Vancouver.

campaign and travelled to Parliament to lobby successfully for changes in federal food testing regulations.[5]

Immigration was another battlefront. In February 1975, Ottawa issued a Green Paper asking Canadians to discuss the nation's immigration policy. Chinese organizations in Vancouver formed a coalition, held public meetings, and convened a Chinese-Canadian national conference on the issue. Many people attacked the Green Paper as an attempt to blame immigrants for the country's rising unemployment, inflation, and housing shortages. They called instead for the government to reaffirm its commitment to multiculturalism and the universality principle in immigration laws.

The face of racism had changed. Discrimination in work or housing could be redressed through human rights legislation. The 1971 federal multiculturalism policy and the race relations initiatives of city hall and the Vancouver School Board proclaimed that visible minorities should stand

Names in the News: Businessmen

North America makes heroes out of its millionaires, and Vancouver has a large number of successful Chinese-Canadian businessmen. These four received substantial press attention.

David Lam

David Lam moved to Vancouver in 1967 with his wife and three young daughters. In Hong Kong he had been chief executive officer of the Ka Wah Bank, but here he went to work in real estate. He helped form Vancouver's Hong Kong Merchants' Association. Lam retired at age sixty, determined to give away his fortune. The University of British Columbia, the University of Victoria, the evangelical Christian Regent College, and the Dr. Sun Yat-sen Garden have each received one million dollars from him.

"I carry this burden, that I want Canadians to recognize that the Chinese in this country are not a liability. Otherwise, I would be quite happy just sailing and digging my garden. People from Hong Kong bring entrepreneurship and a hard-working spirit. But whether the Oriental presence is going to be easily accepted is another matter. One can easily legislate against discrimination, but no one can legislate love."[11]

David Lam at the Chinese Cultural Centre, 1987.

proud of their heritage, but legislation alone could not kill racism.

The media continued to project inaccurate and often damaging images of Chinese Canadians.

One such storm occurred in July of 1979 when Canada's National Film Board (NFB) released a documentary, *Bamboo, Lions and Dragons*. The film tried to examine Vancouver's Chinese history by profiling two families. But when community representatives previewed the film, they immediately denounced it as inaccurate and racist. One line in the script said the Chinese were lucky their food appealed to whites because the Chinese had gained acceptance through the stomach! The NFB halted distribution of the film and agreed to make corrections.

Another storm, national in scope, erupted after the CTV national news-magazine program "W5" aired "The Campus Giveaway" on 30 September 1979. The segment alleged that Canadian taxpayers were subsidizing foreign students while

Canadians were denied an education. Throughout the program, each time the words "foreign students" came up, the screen showed Chinese faces. The message was clear: Chinese Canadians were foreigners, even if they were born here or had acquired citizenship. In April 1980 CTV finally issued an unequivocal apology in a press release:

Although it was never our intention to produce a racist program, there is no doubt that the distorted statistics combined with our visual presentation, made the program appear racist in tone and effect. We share the dismay of the critics that this occurred. We sincerely apologize for the fact that Chinese Canadians were depicted as foreigners, and for whatever distress this stereotyping may have caused them in the context of our multicultural society.

In 1985 there was a local outcry against *The Year of the Dragon*, a major Hollywood film with portrayals of sinister and violent Chinese crime networks in North America.

Chinese Canadians knew that

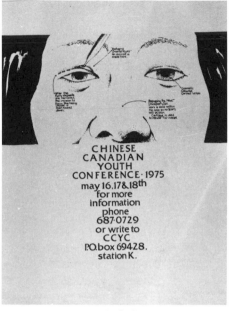

Youth Conference Poster, 1975. By the 1970s, young Chinese Canadians were asking if members of their generation were trying too hard to "fit in."

Tong Louie

Tong Louie was appointed to the board of directors of the Royal Bank of Canada in 1979. Louie, a Vancouver-born University of British Columbia graduate, is chairman and chief executive officer of H. Y. Louie Company Limited, a long-time Vancouver firm, and chairman, president and chief executive officer of London Drugs Limited. In 1985 Louie became the first Canadian to receive the Golden Heart Community Achievement Award from Variety Club International. He was also director of the United Way of the Lower Mainland, a trustee of St. Paul's Hospital, and a member of the board of the YMCA. His firms have sponsored Vancouver Symphony Orchestra performances and a child identification program. He comments on community involvement: "You don't keep on taking things out of the community without giving something back. If you don't keep the symphony alive, Vancouver will become a third-rate city. I'm a Vancouverite, and I'm proud of that! I serve on different boards, I go out and fund raise and sometimes it's tough. But I don't want a public profile. Ours is a family-owned company; we don't have shareholders who want to see the name everywhere."

Ron Shon

Ron Shon took charge of his family's real estate and property management empire in 1977 and tripled its value by 1986. Shon's mother was born in Vancouver but returned to China at the age of two with her parents. Over the years, the family resettled in Vancouver and the Shon Group of companies moved its base here. Shon notes that "My family may have brought

The Dragon Boat Races started in 1986 and attracted teams from corporate, recreational, and community sponsors. The winning team was sent to compete in the Hong Kong International Dragon Boat Races.

At a street performance of martial arts
during one of the Chinese Cultural Centre
festivals (c. 1974), Wong Lung, a long-time
resident of the community, gave an
impromptu demonstration of his technique.

.....

162

Ramona Mar (*centre*) in a scene from the
educational video made at the *Saltwater City*
exhibition at the Chinese Cultural Centre,
1986.

racism still existed in Vancouver. In
1981 and 1986, young Chinese
Canadians complained that downtown
discotheques blocked their entry
because "You orientals don't drink very
much." During the 1987 immigration
debate revived after two boatloads of
Asian immigrants arrived off the
Atlantic coast, former B.C. Supreme
Court Judge J. V. Clyne was upset when
he was labelled a racist for saying that
he wanted to see Canada's culture
remain white. He replied, "You're
bound to be accused of being racist in
trying to maintain a balance for our own
country."[6]

Chinese Canadians also knew that
times had never been better. Most of
those from the second, third, and fourth
generations had good friends who were
white. Interracial marriages were more
common. The governments funded
language, job-training, and seniors'
activity programs. The United Way of
Vancouver backed SUCCESS, which had
satellite offices serving immigrants who
did not live near Chinatown. Local

television and radio now broadcast
community news and information, as
well as programming from Asia.

If acceptance was at hand, why did
the concept of community continue?
Because Chinese Canadians stood
physically distinct and could never
vanish into the white mainstream.
Because inequities persisted, and new
immigrants needed help. The media
continued to portray Chinese Canadians
as exotic foreigners. There were calls to
keep Canada white.

Not every Chinese Canadian saw
these issues the same way. Their
viewpoints reflected the era when they
arrived, their social and economic rank,
and their political consciousness. There
were newcomers struggling with
language and jobs. There were those
who did not live this daily struggle but
who extended professional or volunteer
time to help. And there were those who
had graduated successfully from
schools unscathed by racism. The
reasons for the need of many of these
people to belong to a community varied:

---

its initial investment from the
Orient, but we've made most
of our money here. We've paid
Canadian taxes for a long time
now, so it's Canadian money
we're talking about."

In 1984 Shon became
chairman of the Dr. Sun Yat-
sen Garden Society, which
operates the classical gardens
in the heart of Vancouver's
Chinatown. "The gardens are
something that all Chinese
Canadians can be proud of, no

Ron Shon at the Dr. Sun Yat-sen Classical
Garden, 1987.

matter where they come
from," he said. "It's something
purely Chinese that we've
created for future generations,
despite our community
becoming very Canadian."

In 1987 the Downtown
Vancouver Association gave
the garden its Achievement
Award for its "outstanding
contribution to the quality and
character of downtown
Vancouver."[12]

Milton K. Wong

Milton K. Wong's touch
with pension funds has been
described as magic. In 1986 his
company managed, in whole
or in part, more than seventy
major pension funds worth a
total of three billion dollars.

Wong was born in
Vancouver in 1939 to a family
that ran a tailor shop in
Chinatown. After graduating
from the University of British
Columbia, he joined National

Trust in 1963 and worked in its Toronto and Winnipeg offices before returning to Vancouver in 1969. Wong started his own firm, M. K. Wong and Associates Limited, in May 1980. In six years' time, his company became the second-largest pension fund firm in British Columbia.

Wong had started playing the stock market during his university days. "My brother gave me seven thousand dollars and within one year it was down to two thousand. I'll always remember buying Hawker Siddeley at seven dollars and watching it go down to three. That was the best lesson my family ever gave me. It taught me that investing in the stock market is a very difficult thing."

Wong, whose firm is a major supporter of the Dragon Boat Races, funded a 1986 film based on the Chinese Cultural

Milton K. Wong at the Dragon Boat Races, 1987.

Centre's *Saltwater City* exhibition, a 1987 TV documentary on Chinese-Canadian women, and a video on the Asian- and Native-Canadian Panel at the 1987 Asia Pacific Festival.[13]

Saltwater City was a multimedia exhibition that explored one hundred years of Vancouver's Chinese history in celebration of the city's centennial in 1986. Artifacts, costumes, graphics, and vignette settings recreated images of the past. During a three-month run, the show attracted seven thousand visitors.

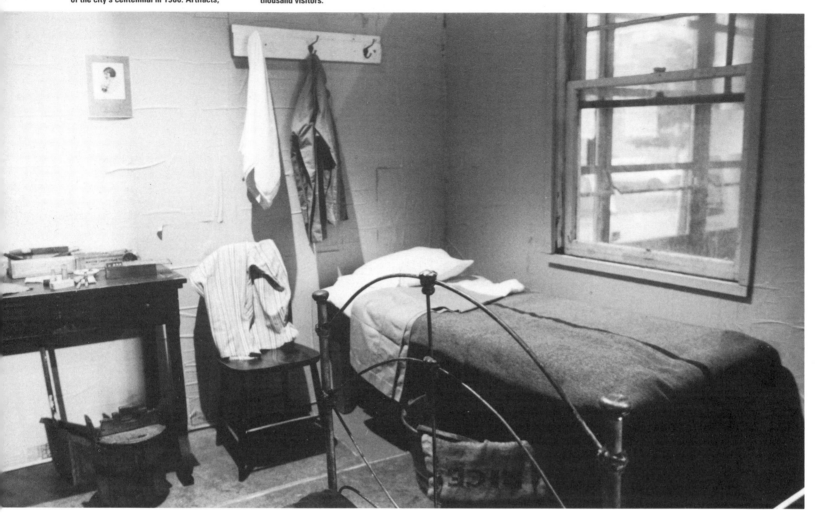

Names in the News: Women

Contemporary Chinese-Canadian women have established themselves as leaders in many professions. Below are five local success stories.

Shirley Chan

When Michael Harcourt was first elected mayor of Vancouver in 1980, he phoned Ottawa to ask Shirley Chan to become his executive assistant. They had met during the urban renewal protests of Strathcona, where Chan had been executive director of the Strathcona Property Owners' and Tenants' Association. She worked at city hall from 1980 to 1986, briefing the mayor on issues, attending meetings, and handling correspondence. In 1982 she told the *Province*: "I'm protected in the sense that I'm a behind-the-scenes person. But I cannot go out in the evening a lot of the time without being in the firing line. People know who you are and they tend to jump on you on an issue. A lot of people want to get something off their chest. On the average day, I leave City Hall between 6 and 7 P.M. I often go on to something else in the evening, whether it's a reception or a meeting. I probably get two nights off a week.[14]

Andrea Eng

Andrea Eng sold forty million dollars' worth of real estate in 1987. She was the sole woman in a staff of forty at Colliers Macaulay Nicolls, a firm specializing in commercial and industrial real estate. When she started she was warned, "We've never had a lady succeed. What makes you think you can do it?"[15] Eng is president of the Hong Kong-Canada Business Association and sits on the City of Vancouver's Economic Advisory Committee.

Lori Fung

Lori Fung won a gold medal in gymnastics at the Los Angeles Olympics in 1984, the first time that rhythmic gymnastics was included in the games. She had been an A student at Vancouver Technical high school when she dropped out to take her grade twelve by correspondence while she trained as a gymnast. At the time of her victory she recalled, "I never had time for a social life or parties in high school, and none of my friends could understand me. But the other day I received a good luck card signed by a lot of the kids I knew in school but whom I hadn't seen in years. They realized what I had been doing all those years and that that dream of mine wasn't so stupid after all."[16]

Angela Kan

In 1986 Hong Kong-born Angela Kan was the second Chinese-Canadian woman to be appointed a judge of the Citizenship Court. She had come to Vancouver after attending the Chinese University of Hong Kong and the University of Chicago, where she completed a Master's degree in sociology. She later received a diploma in Women and Management Studies at Simon Fraser University. In 1977 she became executive director of Vancouver's United Chinese Community Enrichment Services Society, known as SUCCESS.

"There's a very high degree of acceptance and tolerance in Canada. In a lot of European countries, immigrants don't feel they are accepted. We feel at home here. Hong Kong isn't a country, and while we used to sing 'God Save the Queen' in school, it wasn't as if it really

166

移民與土生
"Between Us - Chinese"
A Chinese-Canadian Youth Conference
SAT. FEB. 21, 1976. International House, UBC.
Registration 10:30am or 12:30pm
to examine the gap existing between native-born
and immigrant Chinese-Canadians
Sponsors: Chinese-Canadian Youth Workshop
and Chinese Students' Association, UBC.
Also Art Lee, MP speaks on – 'How well do
Chinese-Canadians work together?'
Art Lee 11:00am   Conference 1:00–5:30

存在的偽膜

"Between Us Chinese," a conference that discussed the gap between Canadian-born and immigrant Chinese Canadians, 1976.

some needed the jobs and doctors of Chinatown, others wanted to resolve the frequent reminders that they looked Chinese.

Today Vancouver's Chinese Canadians can best be seen as a community of communities. They are a monolithic unit only to outsiders who persist in viewing all Chinese Canadians as the same. In reality, there are those who speak no Chinese and others who speak no English; there are the rich and the working class; there are fifth-generation Chinese Canadians, and there are newcomers speaking many languages and dialects. These natural divisions intersect the community. But ultimately, it is like any other Canadian community. The people work, pay taxes, raise families, and hope that the future will shine brighter on everyone.

Two new complexes form the heart of Chinatown today. The Chinese Cultural Centre (CCC) at 50 East Pender Street, supported by traditional associations and newcomer professionals, opened in 1980. It

contains classrooms, a reading room, and exhibition spaces. The adjacent Dr. Sun Yat-sen Garden is the only full-scale Ming dynasty garden outside China. Both institutions sponsor many activities to introduce and interpret aspects of Chinese culture. The crowning achievement of these efforts was the CCC's *Saltwater City* exhibition in 1986, celebrating one hundred years of Chinese life in Vancouver.

had anything to do with us. But now, when we sing 'O Canada,' we are singing about our own country."[17]
Alexina Louie
In 1986 Alexina Louie was one of the few women in Canada who actually made a living as a composer. Born in Vancouver, she studied at the University of British Columbia and in California. She composed "The Ringing Earth," a commission for the gala opening of Expo 86 in Vancouver, while another piece, "The Eternal Earth," was taken by the Toronto Symphony Orchestra as the only Canadian composition on its European tour. In 1986 she was named Composer of the Year by the Canadian Music Council.

"I'm in a very lonely occupation, writing avant-garde music. I was very shy when I was a kid, so I began to

Alexina Louie, 1987.

express myself through the piano, through my music. I put all the torment, joy, and loving I knew into my music. My music made me into a human being. Music is an act of communication. I'm not afraid to cry in my music, or to express the exhilaration of joy."

NOTES

CHAPTER ONE

1 Useful premigration studies include Maurice Freedman, *Lineage Organization in Southeastern China* (London: Athlone Press, 1970); Him Mark Lai and Philip Choy, *Outlines: History of the Chinese in America* (San Francisco, 1973); June Mei, "Socioeconomic Origins of Emigration: Guangdong to California 1850-1882," *Modern China* 5 (October 1979): 463-501.

2 Canada, House of Commons, Royal Commission on Chinese Immigration, "Report and Evidence," 1885 (hereafter cited as 1885 "Report"), p. 77.

3 Edgar Wickberg, ed., *From China to Canada* (Toronto: McClelland and Stewart, 1982), p. 16.

4 John David Adams, "The Rise and Maturation of an Effective Anti-Chinese Argument in British Columbia, 1858-1879" (B.A. Honours paper, University of British Columbia, 1972), p. 22.

5 Robert S. Wynne, "Reaction to the Chinese in the Pacific Northwest Coast and B.C., 1858-1910" (Ph.D. diss., University of Washington, 1964), p. 125.

6 Adams, "Anti-Chinese Argument," p. 24.

7 1885 "Report," p. 152.

8 Wynne, "Reaction to the Chinese," p. 135.

9 Wickberg, *From China to Canada*, p. 19.

10 Paul Yee, "The Chinese in B.C.'s Salmon Canning Industry," in *Inalienable Rice: A Chinese and Japanese Canadian Anthology*. Garrick Chu et al., eds. (Vancouver: Powell Street Revue, 1979).

11 Canada, House of Commons, "Report of Parliamentary Select Committee on Chinese Labour and Immigration," *Journals*, vol. 13 (1879), Appendix 4, 49.

12 1885 "Report," p. 142.

13 Wickberg, *From China to Canada*, p. 24.

14 1885 "Report," p. 56.

15 1885 "Report," p. 65.

16 1885 "Report," p. 56.

CHAPTER TWO

1 Patricia E. Roy, "The Preservation of the Peace in Vancouver: The Aftermath of the Anti-Chinese Riot of 1887," *B.C. Studies* 31 (Autumn 1976): 44-59.

2 Canada, House of Commons, Royal Commission on Chinese and Japanese Immigration, "Report," *Sessional Papers*, 1902, no. 54 (hereafter cited as 1902 "Report"), p. 44.

3 1902 "Report," p. 167.

4 1902 "Report," pp. 188-89.

5 1902 "Report," pp. 188-89.

6 W. Peter Ward, *White Canada Forever* (Montreal: McGill-Queen's University Press, 1978), pp. 19, 169.

7 L. G. Henderson, ed., *Henderson's British Columbia Gazetteer and Directory, 1889* (Victoria, 1889), p. 229.

8 1902 "Report," pp. 178, 182.

9 Medical Health Officer to Royal Commission on Chinese and Japanese Immigration, 15 November 1900, City Clerk's Letters, vol. 17, p. 13298, CVA.

10 Royal Commission to Investigate into Losses Sustained by the Chinese Population of Vancouver, B.C., 1908, William Lyon Mackenzie King Papers, Memoranda and Notes, 1887-1921, vols. C39 to C41, Public Archives of Canada.

11 Paul Yee, "Sam Kee: A Chinese Business in Early Vancouver," *B.C. Studies* 69-70 (Spring-Summer 1986): 93.

12 Dora Anne Nipp, "Canada Bound: An Exploratory Study of Pioneer Chinese Women in Western Canada" (M.A. thesis, University of Toronto, 1983), pp. 29, 40.

13 Nipp, "Canada Bound," pp. 29, 40.

14 J. S. Matthews, "Early Vancouver," vol. 3, p. 217, CVA.

15 Paul Yee, "Chinese Business in Vancouver 1886-1914" (M.A. thesis, University of British Columbia, 1978), pp. 33-37.

16 Vancouver *Daily Province*, 4 June 1908, p. 4; and Vancouver *Daily Province*, 5 June 1908, p. 1.

17 Garnett Weston, "The Last of the Giants," *B.C. Magazine*, vol. 7 no. 8 (September 1911): 895-99.

18 Daphne Marlatt and Carole Itter, comps. and eds., "Opening Doors: Vancouver's East End," *Sound Heritage*, vol. 8 nos. 1 and 2 (1979): 40.

19 1902 "Report," p. 34.

CHAPTER THREE

1 *Census of Canada*, 1921, 1: p. 542.

2 Wickberg, *From China to Canada*, p. 95.

3 By 1923, fifty-two of the city's seventy greengrocers were Chinese. Over half of Vancouver's forty-one Chinese hand laundries were well outside Chinatown. In the restaurant line, twenty-five Chinese took out licences in 1911; six were for Chinese restaurants and the rest were western cafés and coffee houses. By 1923, seventy-five restaurant licences were issued to Chinese and only eighteen were for Chinatown operations. The Chinese-run, Western-style cafés were mostly found in the downtown eastside where waterfront, office and transient workers wanted cheap, quick meals. Licence Registers, 1911, 1923, Department of Permits and Licences, CVA.

4 *Chinese Times*, 21 January 1914.

5 David Lai, "Chinese Attempts to Discourage Emigration to Canada," *B.C. Studies* 18 (Summer 1973): 45-48.

6 *Chinese Times*, 1 February 1915; 26 and 31 January 1916; 12 May 1916.

7 *Chinese Times*, 26 May 1915; 28 June 1916; 16 November 1917.

8 *Chinese Times*, 26 February 1915; 29 June 1922.

9 *Vancouver Daily Province*, 5 June 1922, p. 7.

10 *Vancouver Daily Province*, 28 February 1921, p. 19.

11 *Vancouver Daily World*, 23 January 1922, p. 4.

12 *Vancouver Daily World*, 16 January 1922, p. 4.

13 H. Glynn Ward, *The Writing on the Wall* (Vancouver: Sun Publishing, 1921).

14 *Chinese Times*, 5 January 1921.

15 *Chinese Times*, January 1921 issues.

16 *Chinese Times*, 20 October 1921.

17 *Chinese Times*, 7 September 1920; 13 August 1921.

18 *Chinese Times*, 20 October 1921.

19 *Chinese Times*, 22 January 1920.

20 *Chinese Times*, 10 May 1923.

21 *Chinese Times*, 4 April 1919; 5 March 1920; 26 February 1921.

22 *Chinese Times*, February 1921 issues.

23 *Chinese Times*, 20 June 1918.

24 *Chinese Times*, 10 and 14 June 1919.

25 Wickberg, *From China to Canada*, pp. 108-9.

26 *Chinese Times*, 19 January 1918.

27 *Chinese Times*, 17 September 1914; 24 June 1915; 5 February 1918; 24 December 1923.

28 Harry Chin was interviewed by Philip Shing and Angela Chan for the Chinese Library Services Association, 23 October 1985; Wong Quan was interviewed by Philip Shing for the Chinese Library Services Association, August 1985; Jung Hong-Len was interviewed by Theresa Low for the Provincial Archives of British Columbia, June-July 1980.

29 Wing Wong was interviewed by Jim Wong-Chu and Cindy Chan Piper, 29 July 1977; Wong Quan was interviewed by Philip Shing for the Chinese Library Services Association, August 1985. For Jack Kong, see *Province*, 3, 4, 6 and 16 April 1914.

30 Marlatt and Itter, "Opening Doors," p. 38.

31 Jung Hong-Len was interviewed by Theresa Low for the Provincial Archives of British Columbia, June-July 1980; also *Chinese Times*, July 1917; March-May 1919; February, March, August 1920; January 1921 issues.

32 Leon Ladner quotations are from Canada, House of Commons, *Debates*, 1922, p. 1529, 1530; Neville Lascelles Ward, *Oriental Missions in British Columbia* (New Westminster: Society for Propagation of Gospel in Foreign Parts, 1925), p. 62.

CHAPTER FOUR

1 *Chinese Times*, 2, 20, 21 and 23 June 1924.

2 *Chinese Times*, 20 November 1924; 25 August 1925; 2 December 1926; 9 September 1927; 31 January 1928; 10 February 1931.

3 *Chinese Times*, 16 March 1928.

4 *Chinese Times*, 2 April 1930.

5 Licence Registers, 1923, 1935, Department of Permits and Licences, CVA.

6 Patricia Roy, "Protecting Their Pocketbooks and Preserving Their Race: White Merchants and Oriental Competition," *Cities in the West: Papers of the Western Canada Urban History Conference,* A. R. McCormack and Ian Macpherson, eds. (Ottawa: National Museums of Canada, Mercury Series, History Division no 10, 1975): 117.

7 Roy, "Protecting Their Pocketbooks," p. 123.

8 *Chinese Times,* 21 February 1929.

9 Wickberg, *From China to Canada,* p. 179.

10 *Chinese Times,* 31 January, 26 July, 1 August, 25 September and 18 December 1928.

11 Newsclipping dated 27 August 1935, M1076-1, CVA.

12 Newsclipping dated 9 September 1936, M1076-1, CVA.

13 Newsclipping dated 8 July 1936, M1076-1, CVA.

14 Newsclipping dated 5 September 1936, M1076-1, CVA.

15 Newsclipping dated 9 February 1937, M1076-1, CVA.

16 Newsclippings dated 1, 2 and 3 March 1937, M1076-1, CVA.

17 *Chinese Times,* 11 and 20 October 1924.

18 Lennie Report, 1928, Police Commissioners, 37D12 to 37D18, CVA.

19 Ian Cameron to Police Commission, 21 June 1932, Police Commissioners, General Files, 75C6#4, CVA; also *Chinese Times,* 11 October 1930.

20 Chief Constable to Mayor, 25 July 1933, Police Commissioners, General Files, 75C7#11, CVA.

21 City Council Minutes, 12 November 1935, CVA.

22 Ying Lee was interviewed by Tamara Adilman.

23 Chief Constable to Mayor, 3 September 1937, Mayor's Papers, 33D6#4, CVA.

24 Newsclipping dated 10 February 1937, M6978, CVA.

25 City Council Minutes, 21 September 1937, CVA.

26 Newsclippings dated 29 September and 12 October 1937, M1803-1, CVA; Vancouver Mothers' Council to Mayor, 29 September 1937, City Clerk's Letters, 17A2#8, CVA.

27 *Chinese Times,* 15 November and 1, 2, 5, 8, 9, 10 December 1930.

28 Chinese Benevolent Association to Mayor, 30 Nov 1931, City Clerk's Letters, 15D3#1, CVA.

29 Relief Officer to Relief Committee, 6 June 1932, City Clerk's Letters, 15F1#2, CVA.

30 E. W. Griffith to G. M. Endacott, 24 March 1936, Social Service Department, 106A6#12, CVA.

31 Hilda Hellaby, "Report on Chinese Relief," February 1935, City Clerk's Letters, 16C7#9, CVA.

32 *Chinese Times,* 14 November 1933.

33 Provincial Workers Council to Mayor, 22 January 1935 and Gordon Grant to Mayor, 30 January 1935, City Clerk's Letters, 16D5#3, CVA.

34 *Chinese Times,* 6, 7 and 19 March 1935.

35 Relief and Unemployment Committee Minute Book, vol. 62, p. 117, CVA.

36 *Chinese Times,* 14 December 1935.

37 Social Service Department Minute Book, vol. 64, 4 April 1938, p. 173, CVA.

38 Newsclipping dated 1 September 1938, p. 25, M1803-1, CVA.

39 Newsclipping dated 13 October 1931, M6978; 1 February 1932, M1803-1, CVA.

40 Newsclipping dated 18 September 1937; 7 September 1939; 27 November 1939, M1803-1, CVA.

41 Wickberg, *From China to Canada,* p. 191.

42 Newsclipping dated 27 May 1941, M13,407; 21 March 1942, M1803-2, CVA.

43 Newsclippings dated 23 May 1941 and 16 October 1941, M1803-2, CVA; *News-Herald,* 7 July 1943.

44 *News-Herald,* 22 May 1943.

45 Patricia Roy, "The Soldiers Canada Didn't Want: Her Chinese and Japanese Citizens," *Canadian Historical Review* 54 no. 3 (1978): 351.

46 Newsclipping dated 9 June 1943, M1803-2, CVA.

47 Newsclipping dated 15 June 1944, M1803-2, CVA.

48 Spoon Wong was interviewed by Jim Wong-Chu.

CHAPTER FIVE

1 Newsclipping dated 11 September 1946, M1803-3, CVA.

2 Newsclipping dated 5 December 1946, M1803-3, CVA.

3 Canada, House of Commons, *Debates,* 1947, vol. III, p. 2644-46.

4 *Chinatown,* 3 May 1956.

5 *Maclean's,* 15 January 1949.

6 *New Citizen,* 1 January 1949.

7 *New Citizen,* 13 May 1951.

8 Newsclipping dated 16 February 1948, M1803-4, CVA.

9 *New Citizen,* 1 August 1950.

10 *Chinatown,* 3 July 1956.

11 *Chinatown,* 3 October 1957.

12 *Chinese Times,* 14 October 1949.

13 *Chinese Times,* 26 November 1951.

14 Vancouver *Sun,* 25 August 1962.

15 Vancouver *Sun,* 10 April 1952.

16 Vancouver *Province,* 29 October 1955.

17 Vancouver *Sun,* 24 May 1960.

18 Vancouver *Sun,* 17 July 1961.

19 Vancouver *Sun,* 18 July 1961.

20 Vancouver *Province,* 4 February 1961.

21 Vancouver *Sun,* 19 January 1963.

22 Vancouver *Sun,* 17 October 1967.

23 Vancouver *Sun,* 19 October 1967.

24 Howard Yan and Jim Wong-Chu, "Two Little Wooden Things and a Couple of Strings," Chinese Students Association *Journal,* September 1985, pp. 14-15.

25 Robert McKeown, "How Chinese Are Smuggled into Canada," *Weekend Magazine,* 29 April 1961.

26 Bryce Williams, "House of Twelve Old Men Key to Slum Clearance Fight," Vancouver *Sun,* 7 January 1961.

27 Vancouver *Sun,* 16 July 1962.

CHAPTER SIX

1 Vancouver *Sun,* 15 October 1983.

2 Vancouver *Province,* 16 May 1973.

3 Vancouver *Sun,* 24 October 1973.

4 Vancouver *Province,* 30 January 1971.

5 Vancouver *Province,* 7 October 1972, 28 July 1973; Vancouver *Sun,* 6 June 1978.

6 Vancouver *Sun,* 19 September 1987.

7 All speakers here were interviewed by Ramona Mar for the *Saltwater City* exhibition in 1986.

8 Vancouver *Sun,* 27 January 1973.

9 *The Ubyssey,* 7, 9, 14, 17, 21, 23, 31 March 1978.

10 Vancouver *Province,* 22 November 1967; 13 September 1971; 13 August 1977; 8 December 1977.

11 *Maclean's,* 7 July 1986, p. 37; Vancouver *Sun,* 26 May 1987.

12 *Canadian Business,* May 1987, p. 97.

13 Vancouver *Province,* 27 January 1973.

14 Vancouver *Province,* 2 August 1982.

15 Mia Stainsby, "Wise Words from the Future," Vancouver *Sun: Business Outlook 88* (Winter 1988), p. 10.

16 Vancouver *Sun,* 24 July 1984.

17 *Alumni* (Simon Fraser University journal, Winter 1986/87): 11; Vancouver *Province,* 30 June 1986.

FURTHER READING

170

Adilman, Tamara. "A Preliminary Sketch of Chinese Women and Work in British Columbia 1858-1950." In *Not Just Pin Money: Selected Essays on the History of Women's Work in British Columbia,* edited by Barbara K. Latham and Roberta J. Pazdro, 53-78. Victoria: Camosun College, 1984.

Chan, Anthony B. *Gold Mountain: The Chinese in the New World.* Vancouver: New Star Books, 1983.

Chu, Garrick, et al., eds. *Inalienable Rice: A Chinese and Japanese Canadian Anthology.* Vancouver: Intermedia Press, 1980.

Lim, Sing. *West Coast Chinese Boy.* Montreal: Tundra Books, 1979.

Marlatt, Daphne, and Carole Itter, comps. and eds. "Opening Doors: Vancouver's East End." *Sound Heritage,* vol. 8, nos. 1 and 2 (1979).

Morton, James. *In the Sea of Sterile Mountains.* Vancouver: J. J. Douglas Ltd., 1974.

Roy, Patricia. "White Canada Forever: Two Generations of Studies." *Canadian Ethnic Studies,* vol. 11, no. 2 (1979): 97-109.

Vancouver Art Gallery. *Gum San: Gold Mountain.* Vancouver: Vancouver Art Gallery, 1985.

Ward, W. Peter. *White Canada Forever.* Montreal: McGill-Queen's University Press, 1978.

Wickberg, Edgar, ed. *From China to Canada.* Toronto: McClelland and Stewart, 1982.

Yee, Paul. "Sam Kee: A Chinese Business in Early Vancouver, 1890-1916." In *Vancouver Past: Essays in Social History,* edited by Robert A. J. McDonald and Jean Barman, 70-96. Vancouver: University of British Columbia Press, 1986.

References to main text are in regular type, those to sidebar text are in **bold type**, and those to illustrations are in *italic type*.

ACKNOWLEDGEMENTS

Excerpts from articles in the Vancouver *Province* newspaper (4 June 1908, page 4; 5 June 1908, page 5; 2 March 1937, editorial) reprinted by permission. Excerpt from interview with Chang Yun Ho, Daphne Marlatt and Carole Itter, comps. and eds., "Opening Doors: Vancouver's East End," *Sound Heritage,* vol. 8, nos. 1 and 2 (1979) reprinted by permission of the Provincial Archives of British Columbia, Daphne Marlatt and Carole Itter. Excerpts from articles in the Vancouver *Sun* newspaper (7 January 1961 and 16 July 1962, editorial) reprinted by permission. Excerpts from J.S. Matthews, "Early Vancouver," vol. 3, p. 217, reprinted by permission of Vancouver City Archives. Excerpt from Robert McKeown, "How Chinese Are Smuggled into Canada," *Weekend Magazine,* 29 April 1961, reprinted by permission of Bob McKeown.

Illustrations are listed by page number and location, (t) top, (b) bottom, (l) left and (r) right. Principal sources are credited under the following abbreviations:

--PAC   Public Archives of Canada
--PABC   Provincial Archives of British Columbia
--UBC   University of British Columbia
--VCA   Vancouver City Archives
--VPL   Vancouver Public Library

/8 Peabody Museum of Salem /9 Author's collection /10 Peabody Museum of Salem A9162 /11(t) Larry Wong: (b) PAC C64765 /12 PABC /13 VPL 12866 /14 Glenbow Archives NA3740-29 /15 UBC Main Library /16 VCA Bu.P.403 N.387#1 /17 UBC Main Library /18 PABC HP15252 /19 *Revised Statutes of British Columbia* /20 VPL 6729 /22-23 Lillian Ho Wong /24(t) VPL 35474: (b) *Revised Statutes of British Columbia* /25(t) Vancouver Maritime Museum 1804: (b) VCA /26-27 VCA Mi.P.2 N.26: / 28(t) VPL 3027: (b) PABC HP59641 /29 PAC PA118195 /30 VCA Str.P.232 N.145 /31(t) UBC Special Collections, Cumyow Family Papers: (b) Dr. Wallace Chung /32(tl) VPL 6831: (tr) VCA 287-2: (b) Dr. Wallace Chung /33(l) Private collection: (r) Victoria Yip /34 VPL 5240 /35 A. Jack Lee /36(t) VCA 1901-6: (b) VCA 1901-6 /37(t) VCA 287-4: (b) VCA /38-39 VPL 9498 /40(t) *Henderson's Directory*: (m) VCA Add. MSS571, Vol.6, file 7: (b) Chinese Community Library Services Association /41(t) Lillian Ho Wong: (b) VCA Album M14 /42-43 Victoria Yip /44 Vancouver Museum 1-1871 /45 VPL 8587 /46 VPL 26691 /47 Chinese United Church /48 Chinese United Church /50(t) VCA: (b) Harry Chin /51 Elsie Yet /52(t) UBC Special Collections: (b) Dr. Wallace Chung /53(t) Ian Lee: (b) Author's collection /54 Chinese Cultural Centre /55 Henry Yip /56(t) Vancouver Museum: (b) VPL /57 Vancouver Museum /58(l) Elsie Yet: (r)

VPL 58903 /59(l) VPL 58904: (r) Duncan Stacey / 60-61 Vancouver Public Library 58897 /62(t) Author's collection: (b) Paul Yee /63 Gordon Cumyow /64(t) VPL 13876: (bl) Royal British Columbia Museum: (br) UBC Special Collections, Cumyow Family Papers /65 VPL 3542 /66 Gordon Cumyow /67(t) Anna Lam: (b) Lillian Ho Wong /68 Henry Yip /69(t) VPL 2008: (b) Chinese United Church /70 Chinese United Church /71 UBC Special Collections /72 VCA Port.P1893 N479 /74 VCA Re.P.13 76(t) Ian Lee: (b) UBC Main Library / 77 VPL 7921 /78(t) Tommy Ming Lum: (b) Dr. Wallace Chung /79 Tommy Ming Lum /80(b) Paul Yee: /80-81 Elsie Yet /82 VCA Crookall Collection 260-1268 /83(t) VCA: (b) Paul Yee /84 Paul Yee /85 Robert Shun Wong /86 Paul Yee /87(t) VCA Crookall Collection 260-297: (b) Paul Yee /88 VCA Crookall Collection 260-316 /89(t) VCA: (b) Private collection /90 Spoon Wong /91 VPL 8799 /92 Private collection /93 VPL /94 Patrice Chu /95(t) VCA: (b) VCA Bu.P.253 N.158 /96-97 Jack and Bill Wong /98 Herbert Lim /100-101 VCA 492-47 /102 Patrice Chu /103(t) UBC Special Collections: (b) Author's collection /104 Wing Wong /105 Paul Yee / 106 UBC Special Collections, Cumyow Family Papers /107 Author's collection /108 VPL 40636 / 109(t) Larry Wong: (b) Paul Yee /110(t) VPL: (b) Hon Hsing Athletic Association /111 Donna Chan / 112 Larry Wong /113(t) UBC Special Collections: (b) Paul Yee /114(l) PAC 112783: (r) PAC 112784 / 116 VPL /117(t) VPL 2000: (b) VPL 41630 /118(t) VPL: (b) Paul Yee /119 Vancouver School Board K578 /120 VPL 50426 /121 Hon Hsing Athletic Association /122 VPL 40638 /123 Lillian Ho Wong / 124-125 Vancouver School Board K494 /127(t) PAC C45080: (b) Larry Wong /128 VPL 41604 /129(t) Author's collection: (b)Hon Hsing Athletic Association /130(t) VPL 41632: (b) Hon Hsing Athletic Association /131(t) Vancouver School Board K592: (b) Chinese Benevolent Association / 132(t) Larry Wong: (b) Paul Yee /135 VPL 41609 / 136 Jim Wong-Chu /138-139 Jim Wong-Chu /140(t) Romy So: (b) Tommy Tao /141 Jim Wong-Chu /142 Jim Wong-Chu /143(t) Jim Wong-Chu: (b) Jack Say Yee /144(t) John K. Wong: (b) Author's collection / 145 Dr. Sun Yat-sen Garden /146 Shu Tung Wong / 147(t) Jim Wong-Chu: (b) Paul Yee /148(t) Paul Yee: (b) Paul Yee /149(t) Jim Wong-Chu: (b) Paul Yee / 150 VPL 54056C 151(t) Jim Wong-Chu: (b) Paul Yee /152 Author's collection /153(t) Paul Yee: (b) Jim Wong-Chu /154 Paul Yee /155 Jim Wong-Chu / 156(t) Paul Yee: (b) Paul Yee /157 VPL 54060 / 158(t) Author's collection: (b) Paul Yee /159 Author's collection /160 Michael Mong /161 Jeff Yip /162(t) Elwin Yuen: (b) Paul Yee /163(t) Jim Wong-Chu: (b) Paul Yee /164 Paul Yee /165 Paul Yee / 166(t) Author's collection: (b) Paul Yee /167 Paul Yee

枕等符

灶甑怪符

牛犬等符

禽入家符

鳥污冠

此符佩帶大吉

硃書此符貼廚房吉

硃書此符貼怪處吉

硃書此符貼大門吉

硃書此符佩帶

四物具等怪符

鎮舟車等怪速靈符

鎮野獸入人家等符

鎮鵝鵝鳥等怪之符

鎮諸般鵝怪之